Introduction

Freight transport plays a key role in the economy. Over the past several decades, as the U.S. economy and the role of international trade have grown, freight shipping activity has increased substantially. That activity has been accompanied by a considerable amount of public and private spending on the highway and rail infrastructure that supports it.

The economic returns from such investments depend on the public and private value of the activities they support, including freight transport. The returns will be higher to the extent that investments are based on accurate information about value. For freight transport, information for private investments comes from the prices that freight carriers receive and the demand for their transport services at those prices. But because freight-transport prices largely do not reflect the external (or social) costs of those services—including pavement damage, traffic congestion, accident risk, and exhaust emissions of particulate matter (PM) and carbon dioxide (CO_2)—those prices convey inaccurate information about public value.

In particular, the external costs of transport by truck and by rail differ markedly.[1] Thus, their market shares, and the size of the market, differ from what they would be if prices reflected external costs more accurately: More freight is shipped, and more is shipped by truck, than would otherwise occur. As a result, more time is lost to highway congestion, and more resources are devoted to building and maintaining highway capacity and to alleviating the effects of diesel emissions and accidents, than if shippers paid their share of those external costs.

Taxing freight transport on the basis of external costs would cause shippers to "internalize" those costs. The untaxed external costs of truck transport tend to be much higher, per ton-mile, than those of rail transport, even after accounting for the taxes that freight carriers already pay. Taxes that more fully reflected external costs would cause some freight to shift from truck to rail. Because truck and rail are not perfect substitutes, the shift would probably be modest. But it would reduce external costs and allocate resources more efficiently, and the tax revenue could be used to lower other taxes, reduce the deficit, or increase spending for the nation's public transport infrastructure or for other purposes.

This paper provides estimates of the effects of a variety of such taxes. Using a simulation model based on observed overland shipping activity in the United States, the analysis shows how each tax would affect shippers' choice of transport mode and the amounts of carload/truckload, bulk, intermodal freight (which travels by truck and rail), and automobiles that would be shipped. The model's predictions are based on estimates of shippers' sensitivity to changes in transport prices and of goods-producers' sensitivity to changes in commodity prices as the cost of transporting those commodities changes. This paper provides estimates of changes in the number of freight-haul trips, external costs, total fuel savings, and the tax revenue from each policy. The options examined here range from a tax on all external costs to more easily administered extensions of existing taxes that would only partially internalize those costs.

External Costs of Freight Transport

Nearly all of the external costs of freight transport fall in one of five categories: pavement damage, traffic congestion, accident risk, emissions of PM and nitrogen oxides (NO_x), and emissions of carbon dioxide. Rail has much lower external costs per ton-mile, on average, than trucking.[2] Locomotives are much more energy-efficient (per ton-mile) than trucks, so their emissions are much lower. In addition, because trains

---

[1] The modes also differ in the quality of benefits they provide, such as speed of delivery. But those benefits, unlike external costs, tend to be private and thus already reflected in the price of the service.

[2] A ton-mile is a ton (2,000 pounds) of freight hauled one mile, or any combination of (pounds × distance) equaling 2,000, such as 200 pounds of freight hauled 10 miles or 10 tons of freight hauled one-tenth of a mile.

travel on privately owned, dedicated rights-of-way, rail freight causes very little damage to public roads and little traffic congestion except at grade crossings (intersections where a railway line crosses a road at the same level, or grade).

Researchers have studied extensively the magnitude of the external costs in those categories—highway maintenance costs due to pavement damage; value of time lost to traffic congestion; losses from injury, mortality, and property damage due to accidents; the health effects of emissions of PM and NO_x; and damages from CO_2 emissions—and the contributions to those costs of overland freight transport. A 2011 study by the Government Accountability Office (GAO) reviewed estimates of those disparate costs and of total truck and rail freight activity, and from them formulated estimates of external costs *per ton-mile* of freight transport by each mode.[3] This paper uses the findings from that study, along with two other studies pertaining to emissions damages, for the parameter values in the freight simulation model.

In the simulations, each external-cost variable can take a range of possible values, reflecting statistical variation in the source estimates used to define those ranges. (See Table 1.) In each simulation, the model selects a value at random from each range. For most of the parameters, all of the values in their ranges are equally likely to be selected. For damages from CO_2, the probability that a value will be selected for the simulation model depends on how frequently such a value is predicted by climate models; values toward the middle of the range in Table 1 are much more likely to be selected. The results reported later in the paper are averages based on 1,000 random selections of those and other parameter values in the simulation model.

Most of the external costs are only indirectly related to ton-miles. Pavement damage is most directly related but can vary by location based on road attributes. Accidents and traffic congestion are related more closely to miles than to ton-miles, and emissions are related to fuel combustion. The ranges of costs in Table 1 are therefore estimates based on average costs per ton-mile.

On average, the costs in Table 1 add up to about 20 percent of the average price per ton-mile to ship by truck and 11 percent of the average rail rate, after netting out the effect of existing taxes. (In this analysis, the average price to ship by truck, across all markets and types of freight, is 15.6 cents per ton-mile, versus 5.1 cents for rail.) The ratios vary from one market to the next because shipping rates vary by distance and type of service—carload, bulk, intermodal, and automobile transport. (For average shipping rates by mode and type of service, see the appendix.)

In particular, the external costs of pavement damage and traffic congestion are much lower for rail as they occur mainly at grade crossings. Railroad tracks are damaged by wear, but track maintenance is a private cost. The much greater cost of pavement damage caused by heavy trucks is an external cost to the extent

---

[3] Government Accountability Office, *Surface Freight Transportation: A Comparison of the Costs of Road, Rail, and Waterways Freight Shipments That Are Not Passed on to Consumers,* GAO-11-134 (January 26, 2011), www.gao.gov/products/GAO-11-134.

Table 1.
Unpriced External Costs

(2014 cents per ton-mile)

Type of Cost	Truck Costs*	Rail Costs*
Pavement Damage	0.74–0.96	0.05–0.06
Traffic Congestion	0.42–0.90	0–0.03
Accident Risk	0.85–2.28	0.11–0.25
Emissions: PM and NO_x	0.59–0.80	0.13–0.24
Emissions: CO_2[†]	0.02–0.22–0.92	0.007–0.05–0.24
Total	**2.62–5.86**	**0.30–0.82**

Sources: GAO (2011), except: for PM and NO_x, H. Scott Matthews, Chris Hendrickson, and Arpad Horvath, "External Costs of Air Emissions From Transportation," *Journal of Infrastructure Systems* (March 2001), pp. 13–17, www.cmu.edu/gdi/docs/external-costs.pdf (46 KB); for carbon dioxide, U.S. Interagency Working Group on Social Cost of Carbon (IWGSCC), *Technical Update of the Social Cost of Carbon for Regulatory Impact Analysis Under Executive Order 12866* (November 2013), www.whitehouse.gov.

Notes: * = All costs in 2014 cents based on chained PCE price index. Simulated taxes on nonemissions costs are net of existing taxes and fees associated with miles traveled: highway tolls and taxes on truck diesel fuel and new truck tires, and the 0.1¢/gallon tax on rail diesel fuel for the Leaking Underground Storage Tank Trust Fund. See GAO (2011).† = CO_2 costs are drawn from IWGSCC's empirical probability distribution for 2020 using a 3 percent discount rate. Reported values are for the 5th–50th–95th percentiles.

that the damage exceeds what trucking companies pay in taxes.[4] Likewise, railroad companies bear most of the costs of rail traffic congestion themselves, because each company operates mostly on its own track. (Amtrak uses tracks owned by freight-rail companies; its trains may be slowed by freight operations but generally receive priority.) Traffic congestion at grade crossings is a major cost in some locations, particularly in freight-hub cities like Chicago and in port cities like Los Angeles. But because relatively few ton-miles occur near crossings, average rail congestion costs mostly reflect lower costs away from crossings.

Freight trains also pose a much lower accident risk to third parties—even adjusted for severity (rail accidents involve greater quantities of freight and may be more likely to involve hazardous materials)— because trucks share the road with other vehicles. Trucks also lack some of the passive safety controls that trains are required to have. GAO's estimates of noncompensated accident risk (that is, net of insurance premiums) predate the recent rise in rail transport of crude oil from the Bakken formation in North Dakota and of oil sands from Canada and several costly derailments involving petroleum tank cars. However, those developments may have had little effect on rail's average accident risk per ton-mile: Crude oil shipments by rail are very heavy and cover long distances, thus generating many accident-free

---

[4] GAO's pavement-damage estimates are based on the Federal Highway Administration's two most recent highway cost-allocation studies. See Federal Highway Administration, *1997 Federal Highway Cost Allocation Study Final Report*, www.fhwa.dot.gov/policy/hcas/final/index.htm; and *Addendum to the 1997 Federal Highway Cost Allocation Study Final Report* (May 2000), www.fhwa.dot.gov/policy/hcas/addendum.htm. For GAO's additional reliance on a forthcoming FHWA cost-allocation study, see GAO (2011), pp. 31 and 38.

ton-miles, which would hold down the average risk per ton-mile even if several costly accidents occurred. In addition, crude oil shipments still represent only a small share of total rail traffic.

For the three highway-related costs in Table 1—pavement damage, traffic congestion, and accident risk— the lower of each pair of estimates is from GAO, except in the case of truck costs of traffic congestion. Most of the higher estimates in each pair come from the *Handbook of Transport Economics* as cited in GAO (2011).[5] For traffic congestion from heavy trucks, because GAO's estimate exceeds the *Handbook* average cited in GAO (2011), that average provides the lower bound and the GAO estimate the upper bound (though raised by a tenth of a cent because GAO characterizes it as "likely to be conservative.")[6] GAO's (2011) highway-cost estimates are based on studies more recent than those summarized in the *Handbook*—by the Transportation Research Board; the Texas Transportation Institute; the Federal Highway Administration (FHWA); and from the peer-reviewed journal *Transportation Research*—and data from the Bureau of Transportation Statistics and FHWA.[7] The Congressional Budget Office has previously relied on the same FHWA study for its recent analysis of the external costs of highway travel.[8] By drawing estimates from multiple sources, the simulation model is not overly dependent on any one source.

For costs relating to emissions, the model uses median damage estimates from the literature.[9] It does not rely on estimates from GAO (2011), because that source does not estimate CO_2 costs, provides very high estimated costs for PM and NO_x, and uses 2002 emissions data for trucks and locomotives. GAO's (2011) very high estimates for PM and NO_x do not capture actual damages but instead come from a 2002 survey by the Environmental Protection Agency (EPA) of individuals' stated willingness to pay for hypothetical reductions in those emissions.[10] At around 0.9 cents per ton-mile for rail and 4.7 cents per ton-mile for

---

[5] See Mark A. Delucchi and Donald R. McCubbin, "External Costs of Transport in the U.S.," in Andre de Palma and others, eds., *A Handbook of Transport Economics* (Edward Elgar Publishing, 2011), pp. 341–368.

[6] GAO (2011), Table 4 footnote, p. 23.

[7] See Texas Transportation Institute, *A Modal Comparison of Domestic Freight Transportation Effects on the General Public* (February 2012), www.nationalwaterwaysfoundation.org/study/FinalReportTTI.pdf (2.2 MB); David J. Forkenbrock, "Comparison of External Costs of Rail and Truck Freight Transportation," *Transportation Research Part A,* vol. 35 (2001), pp. 321–337; David J. Forkenbrock, "External Costs of Intercity Truck Freight Transportation," *Transportation Research Part A,* vol. 33 (1999), pp. 505–526; and Transportation Research Board, *Paying Our Way, Estimating Marginal Social Costs of Freight Transportation* (July 1996).

[8] Congressional Budget Office, *Alternative Approaches to Funding Highways* (March 2011), www.cbo.gov/publication/22059. That study expresses external costs per mile rather than per ton-mile. The underlying costs used by both studies are the same, however. Figure 3 of that study implies average external costs of around 27 cents per mile for pavement damage from heavy trucks. In the current study, the cost of pavement damage ranges from 0.7 cents to 0.9 cents per ton-mile (in 2009 dollars, as in the earlier study) or around 27 cents per mile for a 17-ton tractor-trailer hauling the median payload of about 16 tons (see Table A-8).

[9] H. Scott Matthews, Chris Hendrickson, and Arpad Horvath, "External Costs of Air Emissions From Transportation," *Journal of Infrastructure Systems* (March 2001), pp. 13–17. To see how estimates of emissions of PM and NOx have been reduced for trucks and locomotives, see Table 16 on page A-1 of Texas Transportation Institute, *A Modal Comparison of Domestic Freight Transportation Effects on the General Public* (February 2012), which compares 2009 estimates with 2005 estimates used in an earlier version of the *Modal Comparison* study published in March 2009.

[10] Environmental Protection Agency, *Final Rulemaking to Establish Light-Duty Vehicle Greenhouse Gas Emission Standards and Corporate Average Fuel Economy Standards: Regulatory Impact Analysis*, EPA-420-R-10-009 (April 2010). Respondents were asked to value hypothetical gains in health and longevity from reduced emissions. GAO noted that EPA had told them the survey estimates "should not be considered completely synonymous with costs" because of the methodology used. (GAO (2011), p. 51.)

trucks, GAO's damage estimates are five to seven times higher than the median damage estimates (0.2 cents and 0.7 cents, per ton-mile, respectively) from the literature.[11] In addition, because GAO's data are from 2002, that analysis does not consider more recent advancements in technology. Since that time, truck-engine manufacturers have developed much cleaner diesel engines in response to substantially tightened EPA emissions standards for PM and NO_x.[12] Those engines are gradually being adopted into truck fleets.[13] In recognition of those issues, the simulation model uses the much smaller values from the literature.

For the cost of CO_2 emissions, the model relies on estimates from the U.S. Interagency Working Group on Social Cost of Carbon (IWGSCC), as CBO has done in recent work.[14] The model selects CO_2 damages from the empirical distribution of IWGSCC's most recent estimates for a 3 percent discount rate.[15] Most of those estimates are between $5 and $45 per ton. In the simulation model, those costs have been converted into cents per ton-mile on the basis of estimated average rates of fuel consumption for the two transport modes.

Existing Policies That Affect Truck and Rail Shipping Costs

Various policies established by the federal government, state governments, and port authorities, and influence the baseline (total ton-miles shipped and the mode choice for each shipment) against which this paper measures the effects (examined in later sections) that certain simulated policies would have on shipping by truck versus rail.

Federal Policies Affecting Trucking

Interstate trucking depends on the National Highway System (NHS), including Interstate and other "principal arterial" highways, for its ability to compete with railroads for long-haul freight. Spending from the highway account of the Highway Trust Fund (HTF) was $45 billion in 2014, primarily for construction and maintenance of the NHS and of bridges on public roadways. The HTF is funded mostly from motor-fuel tax revenues, although the Congress has transferred about $65 billion from other sources (mainly the Treasury's general fund) since 2008 to prevent shortfalls in the HTF.

---

[11] GAO's estimates would dwarf the other external costs in the simulation model: They imply damages of $4 to $7 per gallon of diesel fuel, more than 10 times higher than current federal, state, and local fuel taxes combined. (Author's calculation based on estimated fuel economy of 150 ton-miles per gallon for trucks and 475 for rail. Source for those values noted elsewhere in the paper.)

[12] For changes to the National Ambient Air Quality Standards (NAAQS) for particulate matter, see Environmental Protection Agency, "EPA's Revised Air Quality Standards for Particle Pollution: Monitoring, Designations, and Permitting Requirements" (December 2012), www.epa.gov/pm/2012/decfsimp.pdf.
For revisions to the NAAQS for NO_x, see Environmental Protection Agency, "Fact Sheet: Final Revisions to the NAAQS for Nitrogen Dioxide" (January 2010), www.epa.gov/airquality/nitrogenoxides/pdfs/20100122fs.pdf.

[13] For emissions reductions and adoption rates, see Diesel Technology Forum, "New Diesel Truck and Bus Engines Emissions Dramatically Cleaner Than Expected" (December 4, 2013), www.dieselforum.org/index.cfm?objectid=939AACE0-5CF4-11E3-B096000C296BA163.

[14] Interagency Working Group on Social Cost of Carbon, *Technical Update of the Social Cost of Carbon for Regulatory Impact Analysis Under Executive Order 12866* (November 2013), www.whitehouse.gov.
See also Congressional Budget Office, *Effects of a Carbon Tax on the Economy and the Environment* (May 2013), www.cbo.gov/publication/44223.

[15] That empirical distribution comprises estimates from 15,000 model runs (results provided to author by EPA) and is given in Figure 1 ("Distribution of SCC Estimates for 2020") in Interagency Working Group on Social Cost of Carbon, *Technical Support Document: Technical Update of the Social Cost of Carbon for Regulatory Impact Analysis Under Executive Order 12866* (November 2013), www.whitehouse.gov.

The freight trucking industry contributes around one-third of the annual revenue credited to the Highway Trust Fund. In 2014, 24 percent of HTF revenues came from the 24.4¢/gallon federal tax on diesel fuel, most of it paid by freight trucks, which consume about nine-tenths of that fuel. In addition, around 13 percent of the HTF's 2014 revenues were from federal excise taxes on freight trucks, tires, and trailers and from the annual heavy-vehicle use tax. (The Highway Trust Fund receives most of its revenue—63 percent in 2014—from taxes on motor gasoline.) Railroads are currently exempt from federal excise taxes on diesel fuel, other than an assessment of 0.1¢/gallon for the Leaking Underground Storage Tank Trust Fund.

The trucking industry's tax contribution to federal expenditures on public highways is greater than its share of miles traveled on that system—around 14 percent on rural roads and 9 percent overall.[16] But heavy trucks are responsible for a disproportionate share of highway maintenance and repair costs because they are a leading source of pavement damage.[17] The FHWA concluded in 2000 that heavy trucks pay substantially less than their full share of federal highway costs.[18] The external cost estimates in Table 1 reflect that finding—that is, those estimates are net of taxes paid.

Federal Policies Affecting Rail

The Federal Railroad Administration is authorized to provide up to $35 billion in direct loans and loan guarantees for railroads to develop their infrastructure or to refinance existing debt incurred for that purpose. The program has issued roughly $2 billion in loans so far, some of which have gone to freight railroads. The Moving Ahead for Progress in the 21st Century Act authorized $0.22 billion of annual federal spending to improve rail-highway grade crossings. Regional (short line) railroads were able to receive federal tax credits of 50 percent of qualified track-maintenance expenditures, up to $3,500 per track mile, before the program expired at the end of 2013.

The Department of Transportation's TIGER (Transportation Investment Generating Economic Recovery) grant program, initially authorized in the American Recovery and Reinvestment Act of 2009, has distributed more than $100 million to freight-rail infrastructure projects, as well as to other types of transportation projects. In 2013, rail-related TIGER grants ranging from $1.8 million to $14.4 million were used for rail improvements in several states. TIGER grants of similar size were awarded for improvements in intermodal freight handling at several seaports and at the Oklahoma City Intermodal Transportation Hub. Smaller TIGER grants were given for freight-rail improvements in a few other states and at the Container Export Rail Facility in Tucson.

Those various programs ultimately reduce rail freight shipping costs, encouraging shippers to choose rail. But the combined expenditures for those programs—a small fraction of the authorized amount in the case of the loan and loan-guarantee programs—are an order of magnitude less than federal highway expenditures net of fuel taxes.[19] On net, the combination of existing federal policies pertaining to the National Highway System and to rail infrastructure draw some freight business from rail to trucking.

---

[16] Author's calculations based on Federal Highway Administration, *Highway Statistics 2013*, Table VM-1, www.fhwa.dot.gov/policyinformation/statistics/2013/vm1.cfm.

[17] Federal Highway Administration, *1997 Federal Highway Cost Allocation Study Final Report* (2007), www.fhwa.dot.gov/policy/hcas/final/index.htm; and *HVUT Helps Level the Playing Field*, www.fhwa.dot.gov/policy/091116/03.htm.

[18] Federal Highway Administration, *Addendum to the 1997 Federal Highway Cost Allocation Study Final Report* (May 2000), www.fhwa.dot.gov/policy/hcas/addendum.htm.

[19] Congressional Budget Office, *The Highway Trust Fund and the Treatment of Surface Transportation Programs in the Federal Budget* (June 2014), www.cbo.gov/publication/45416.

State Taxes

States vary considerably in their approaches to taxing freight transport. The list of state policies described in this section is not comprehensive: It is limited to the policies that this analysis used as models for several simulated policies.

In addition to the 24.4¢/gallon federal tax on (nonrailroad) diesel fuel, every state plus the District of Columbia imposes its own tax on that fuel, at rates ranging from 11.8¢/gallon in Alaska to 64.2¢/gallon in Pennsylvania. In most states, the tax is a combination of an excise tax and other taxes and fees (in some cases including a percentage sales tax that may vary by location). The average state tax on diesel fuel is about 30¢/gallon.[20]

Certain states also impose weight-distance (WD) taxes on heavy trucks traveling within those states, or a tax on vehicle miles traveled (VMT). WD taxes are used in New Mexico, New York, and Oregon. Only Kentucky imposes a VMT tax on heavy trucks. Other states have tried both types of taxes "but have discontinued them due to collection expense, compliance costs imposed on carriers, legal challenges, and concerns over the impact on state economic development and competitiveness," according to a report published by the Transportation Research Board (TRB).[21]

The WD tax rates in New Mexico and New York are 4.378 cents and 5.46 cents per mile, respectively, for trucks rated at 78,000 pounds or more.[22] Oregon's WD tax rate for large trucks is substantially higher at 16.38 cents per mile in 2012, although Oregon does not tax truck diesel fuel. All three states' WD taxes apply to trucks' *rated* capacities regardless of the weight of their cargo—although for unladen miles, New York imposes a lower rate of around 3.5 cents per mile on the largest trucks. Because those taxes do not otherwise vary with payload weight, they have lower administrative costs than they would otherwise have because they can be assessed on the basis of periodic odometer readings rather than on the waybills for every shipment.

Kentucky's VMT tax is a version of the WD tax that requires less information: It depends only on miles traveled, not on weight or a truck's rated capacity. Kentucky's VMT tax rate is a uniform 2.85 cents per mile on all trucks weighing at least 60,000 pounds including cargo.[23]

Port Container Fees

Certain ports impose fees on container freight to finance the construction of local freight infrastructure or to reduce congestion and emissions. Some fees do not depend on whether the container is shipped by truck or by rail. For example, the Ports of Los Angeles and Long Beach, which handle more containers than any other U.S. port, assess an air-quality charge of $60 per 40-foot container (or FEU, for forty-foot-equivalent unit). The Ports of New York and New Jersey impose a container fee of $63.06 to finance the Millennium Marine Rail, the ports' container-handling facility.[24] Other port fees are mode-specific and could influence some shippers' mode choices—although that effect would probably be small, because the

---

[20] American Petroleum Institute, *State Motor Fuel Taxes* (revised February 12, 2015), www.api.org.

[21] National Cooperative Freight Research Program, *Report 15: Dedicated Revenue Mechanisms for Freight Transport Investment* (2012), p. 49, http://onlinepubs.trb.org/onlinepubs/ncfrp/ncfrp_rpt_015.pdf (12.5 MB).

[22] Although those tax rates do not vary by weight within weight classes, this paper describes those taxes as weight-distance taxes because their rates do vary across weight classes. For information on the states' WD taxes, see National Cooperative Freight Research Program, *Report 15*, pp. 50–51.

[23] Ibid.

[24] Millennium Marine Rail, *ExpressRail Elizabeth Terminal Schedule* (September 17, 2013), www.millenniummarinerail.com.

fee differences are minor compared with total shipping costs. The Ports of Los Angeles and Long Beach also impose a fee of $43.20 per FEU for rail access to the Alameda Corridor, or a fee of $123 per FEU for peak-period truck access to deliver containers to the ports' loading facilities.[25] And the Port of Tacoma charges railroads $20 per container for infrastructure improvements in Washington's FAST Corridor.

A recent report by the National Surface Transportation Policy and Revenue Study Commission recommended that the Congress consider implementing a national overland container fee (or a surcharge on freight waybills) as a way to finance freight infrastructure projects that would remediate traffic chokepoints.[26] The commission recommended that any such fee be accountable and transparent and that revenues be used on projects that would benefit payers by improving freight flows. A report by the National Cooperative Freight Research Program concluded that although a port container fee on international freight would not be a viable option for funding projects of such scope, a more broadly based container fee could be.[27]

Modeling the Effects of Policy Changes on Freight Transport

This paper simulates increases in taxes on overland freight transport to determine the resulting reductions in external costs and fuel consumption, changes in the market shares for each mode, and increases in government revenue. Imposing external-cost taxes on freight carriers would raise shipping rates as carriers passed most or all of those costs along to their customers. In most markets—defined here as the transport of a particular type of commodity from a specific origin state to a specific destination state—truck rates would increase by more than rail rates would. In response, freight customers would shift some of their business from truck to rail, and they would ship slightly less freight overall because all rates would go up.

Previous Research

How mode choice in freight transport would respond to changes in shipping rates has been studied extensively. In the 1970s, with policymakers considering deregulating rail rates, researchers empirically analyzed how shippers' choices between truck and rail are affected by changes in price, in order to anticipate how deregulation would affect freight transport. Those studies tended to find that although deregulation might induce substantial shifts from trucking to rail in some markets, effects in other markets would be small because shippers in those markets are strongly committed to one mode—be it rail or truck—over the other.[28]

More recently, researchers and policymakers have shown interest in shippers' mode choices because of the implications for emissions, traffic congestion, and spending on infrastructure, recognizing that freight

---

[25] For rail fee, see Alameda Corridor Transportation Authority, *Schedule of Use Fees and Container Charges, Effective January 1, 2013,* www.acta.org. For truck "PierPass" fee, see PierPass, "Marine Terminal Operators at the Ports of Los Angeles and Long Beach to Adjust TMF on August 1" (press release), http://pierpass.org/news-room/.

[26] National Surface Transportation Policy and Revenue Study Commission, *Transportation for Tomorrow,* vol. 1 (December 2007) , p. 42, http://transportationfortomorrow.com/final_report/.

[27] National Cooperative Freight Research Program, *Report 15*, *Dedicated Revenue Mechanisms for Freight Transport Investment* (Transportation Research Board, 2012), http://onlinepubs.trb.org/onlinepubs/ncfrp/ncfrp_rpt_015.pdf (12.5 MB).

[28] See Richard C. Levin, "Allocation in Surface Freight Transportation: Does Rate Regulation Matter?" *Bell Journal of Economics,* vol. 9 (1978), pp. 18–45; Tae Hoon Oum, "A Cross Sectional Study of Freight Transport Demand and Rail-Truck Competition in Canada," *Bell Journal of Economics,* vol. 10 (1979), pp. 463–482; and Clifford Winston, "A Disaggregate Model of the Demand for Intercity Freight Transportation," *Econometrica,* vol. 49, no. 4 (July 1981), pp. 981–1006.

rates do not reflect external costs. Those issues were cited in studies of freight transport mode-choice conducted for the Department of Energy, the Departments of Transportation in Virginia and Florida, the Interstate-95 Corridor Coalition, and in Europe.[29] Each of those studies examined the potential of a variety of policies to induce shifts from truck to rail. Policies examined included external-cost taxes, public investments in rail capacity, and subsidies to encourage the use of "excess" rail capacity. One of the studies in particular, although based on data for Europe, produced results similar to the findings in this paper: That study concluded that external-cost pricing would raise truck shipping rates by 8 percent to 25 percent and would cause 2 percent to 8 percent of road transport to shift to rail.[30]

Simulation Model

As in that literature, this paper examines the effects of freight transport policies by estimating how the policies would change shipping rates and then applying those changes to price elasticities to predict how shippers' mode choices would be affected. As explained more fully in the appendix to this paper, the model performs two calculations. One calculation is the change in demand for each commodity—less than 1 percent in most cases—in each transport market because of higher shipping rates.[31]

The other calculation is the resulting shift from truck to rail, measured in ton-miles of freight transport, as rail becomes relatively less expensive because of the policy.[32] In markets where trucking has a smaller share than rail, the shift cannot exceed the total ton-miles by truck in that market.

The model considers each transportation market separately. The unit of observation is annual ton-miles for each state-level origin/destination/commodity, in total and by transport mode. The data include 39 types of commodities and 48 states (Alaska and Hawaii are excluded) plus the District of Columbia. Thus, there are up to 39 observations for every origin-destination state pair. (There would be fewer than 39 observations if not all commodities were transported between those states.) Flows of commodities from,

---

[29] See Cambridge Systematics, *Freight Transportation Modal Shares: Scenarios for a Low-Carbon Future* (report prepared for the Department of Energy, March 2013), www.nrel.gov/docs/fy13osti/55636.pdf (2.9 MB); CE Delft/TRT, *Potential of Modal Shift to Rail Transport* (March 2011), http://cedelft.eu/publicatie/potential_of_modal_shift_to_rail_transport/1163; Cambridge Systematics, *Mid-Atlantic Rail Operations Phase II Study* (report prepared for I-95 Corridor Coalition, December 2009), www.i95coalition.org/i95/Portals/0/Public_Files/pm/reports/MAROps%20Phase%20II%20Final%20Report.pdf (5.8 MB); Virginia Department of Transportation, *Freight Diversion and Forecast Report* (2004), www.virginiadot.org/projects/resources/freight.pdf (2.6 MB); and University of Florida, *The Response of Railroad and Truck Freight Shipments to Optimal Excess Capacity Subsidies and Externality Taxes* (report prepared for Florida Department of Transportation, September 2002), www.dot.state.fl.us/rail/Publications/Studies/Planning/FreightResponseToSubsidyandTax.pdf (310 KB).

[30] The range of possible effects reflects only variation in baseline shipping rates across markets; it does not account for uncertainties in the values of the underlying parameters. See CE Delft/TRT, p. 38.

[31] That calculation is ($\eta \times C \times T$), where η is the own-price elasticity of demand for the commodity; C is that market's percentage change in shipping costs by mode, and T is the transport cost share for that commodity, or the ratio of its transport costs to its total production and distribution costs.

[32] That calculation is approximately ($R_c \times \varepsilon_{r,t}$), where R_c is the relative increase in total shipping costs by truck versus rail, and $\varepsilon_{r,t}$ is the shipper's cross-price elasticity of rail transport, now relatively less costly, with respect to truck transport. So if truck shipping costs in a particular market increased by 10 percent relative to rail, and if the cross-price elasticity was 0.5, rail ton-miles would rise by around 5 percent in that market, with a matching decrease in the number of truck ton-miles. (For short-haul markets, the simulation model uses much smaller elasticities than it does for long-haul markets, recognizing that mode-switching is unlikely to occur in those markets because trucking usually provides much faster service than rail over shorter distances. See footnote 60 for the model's mode-choice elasticities in short-haul markets.)

say, California to Tennessee are counted separately from those from Tennessee to California. In all, the data comprise nearly 76,000 observations.

The model summarizes changes in rail and truck ton-miles at the national level. Using those results, along with estimates of mode fuel efficiency, average payloads, and external costs per ton-mile, the model calculates annual fuel savings, reductions in external costs, changes in the number of individual trips by truck or railcar, and tax revenue from each simulated policy. The analysis is primarily based on data from the 2007 Commodity Flow Survey, part of the Census Bureau's quinquennial Economic Census (see the appendix). (Data from the 2012 survey were released in December 2014, after the analysis in this paper was completed.) The analysis estimates what would have occurred in 2007 had the simulated policies already been in place. (Initial short-term transitions in response to the policies would have occurred before 2007.) Because the data are from 2007, they were not affected by the recession of 2008 and 2009. In estimating tax revenues and other outputs, the analysis does not attempt to project how conditions might change in future years.

Graphically, the new transport prices and quantities resulting from the application of a simulated policy reflect a shift in the demand for each transport mode (truck or rail) from the change in the other mode's prices, and the tax "wedge" between the new prices paid by shippers and the new prices received by carriers. (See Figure 1; the original prices and quantities (p_0, q_0) and the new values (p_1, q_1) correspond to the points labeled 'a' and 'b', respectively, in the figure.)

The simulation model contains many parameters whose values must be specified. In addition to external costs, the model's other parameters are shipping rates (prices), demand elasticities, mode-choice elasticities, and transport cost shares (all of which can vary widely by commodity), drayage (truck-delivery) costs, lift costs (for placement of shipping containers on trucks and rail cars), route distances, and payload capacities. (See the appendix for descriptions of those parameters.) As with external costs, each parameter can take a range of possible values around its average, reflecting statistical variation in the underlying estimates. In most cases, each value within a range is equally likely to be selected. For drayage costs, as for CO_2, the model gives greater probability to midrange values.

Policy Options to Account for the External Costs of Freight

This paper examines three sets of policy options that would tax truck and rail freight on the basis of their external costs net of current taxes. The first set of options would impose external-cost taxes based on the weight and/or distance of each shipment or on the amount of fuel used. The option that would require administrators of the tax to have both weight and distance information about each shipment could be costly to implement. But the analysis of that option provides a useful benchmark against which to compare the other policies, because the weight-and-distance tax is the most closely linked to the market distortions from unpriced external costs.

A second set of options would impose taxes on container shipments. The container taxes analyzed in this paper include a tax based on weight and distance shipped; a uniform tax regardless of weight or distance; and a tax based on distance zones traveled. Finally, grouped by itself, one option would increase the excise tax on truck tires.

Figure 1.
Effect of External-Cost Taxes on Demand for Freight Transport

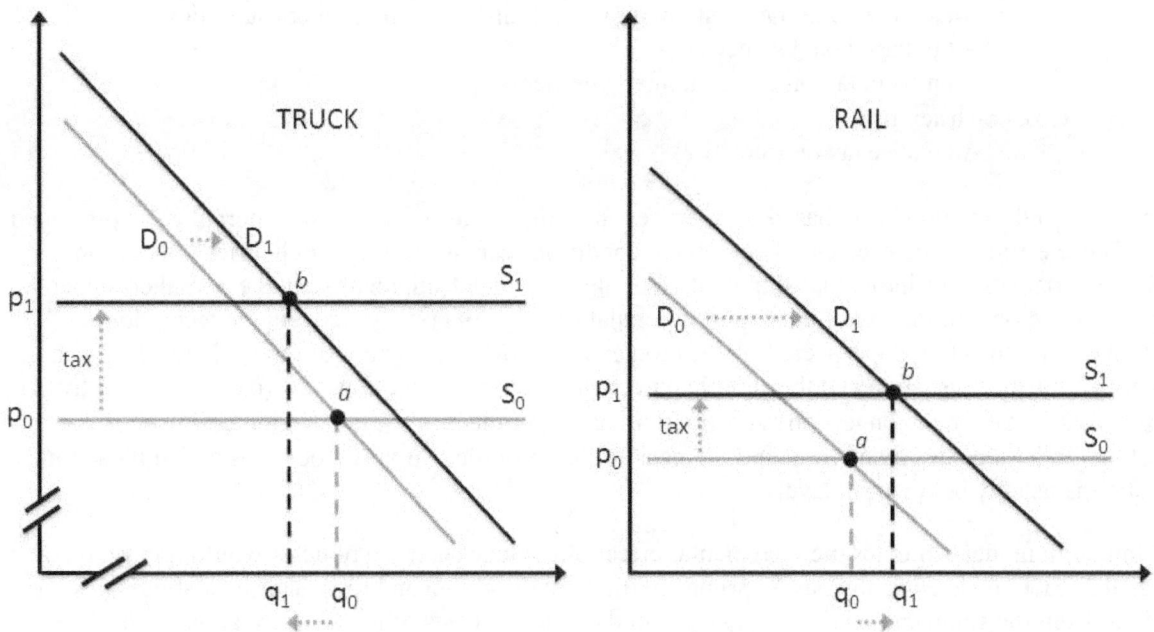

Notes: In both panels, the tax shifts the supply curve from S_0 to S_1 so that the price p_1 that a shipper pays exceeds the price p_0 that the freight-carrier receives by exactly the amount of the tax. In the 'TRUCK' panel, the shift in the demand curve from D_0 to D_1 is in reaction to the increase in the cost of rail shipping, which causes shippers to demand more trucking services at any given price. In the 'RAIL' panel, the demand curve shifts in response to the increase in truck shipping costs. In both panels, points 'a' and 'b' indicate where supply and demand are in balance, respectively, before and after the taxes are imposed.

Because their magnitudes differ sufficiently, the taxes on truck and rail transport have opposite effects: Despite the increase in demand for trucking services, total truck ton-miles decline from q_0 to q_1 in the 'TRUCK' panel. Most of those ton-miles shift to rail, and rail ton-miles increase from q_0 to q_1 in the 'RAIL' panel. Because higher prices for both modes cause a slight decrease in total shipping, the net increase in rail shipping is slightly smaller than the decrease in truck shipping.

The supply of freight transport services is depicted as perfectly price-elastic in both panels, meaning more freight could be hauled without increasing unit costs. That description seems to fit the trucking industry, because additional trucks and drivers can be added relatively easily and current highway capacity can accommodate many more trips (although congestion would increase on some routes). In the rail industry, cars can be added to some (but not all) existing trains, but adding locomotives and engineers is more costly than adding trucks and drivers, and there may be less excess capacity on the industry's track networks than on the nation's highways. Those factors suggest that the rail supply curve may slope upward. In that case, railroad companies would pass along less than 100 percent of the tax to their customers. The simulation model therefore uses a rail tax "pass-through rate" (the portion of the tax that the shippers pay) of between 90 percent and 100 percent—consistent with a slightly upward-sloping supply curve—and selects values at random from within that range. (The model uses a truck tax pass-through rate of 100 percent.)

Each option differs in its trade-off between how effectively it captures external costs and how costly it is to administer. The specific options are as follows:

- Taxes on all freight shipments, based on weight, distance, or fuel consumption
    1. An average-external-cost tax: a weight-and-distance tax plus a fuel tax
    2. A tax on vehicle miles traveled plus a fuel tax: shipment weight not taxed

3. A tax on vehicle miles traveled only
4. A fuel tax only
- Taxes on container shipments (that is, intermodal freight)
  5. An average-external-cost tax on weight, distance, and fuel consumption
  6. A tax based on distance zones
  7. A uniform tax on any container shipment
- Taxes on truck tires
  8. An excise tax on truck tires

The tax rates in those options are based on averages from the ranges of estimated external costs presented earlier. Those estimates themselves reflect typical conditions across all freight deliveries rather than specific external costs for individual shipments. For any individual shipment, actual external costs per ton-mile depend on terrain, size of the exposed population, type of conveyance, engine technology, condition of equipment, and—especially—location and time of day, because of their relationship with costly urban traffic congestion and the significant contribution of freight transport (particularly by truck) to those costs.[33] Although congestion is costly in urban areas, the average congestion cost used in the simulation model includes many rural and off-peak urban ton-miles; in those locations and at those times, congestion is usually below peak levels.

The simulation model estimates the incremental effect of the taxes that the policies would impose relative to taxes that each mode currently pays—primarily truck taxes on fuel and tires. Those existing taxes are netted out from the simulated taxes. Thus, although the external costs of trucking are about eight times greater per ton-mile than those of rail, in the simulations the ratio of the two modes' external-cost taxes is 6 to 1. (See Table 2.)

As Figure 1 shows, carriers would respond to the taxes by increasing the rates they charge shippers (which would, in turn, boost the prices charged to consumers of the shipped goods). Competition in the railroad industry tends not to be as strong in most markets as it is in the trucking industry. In such markets, the railroad companies may not fully pass along a tax to their shippers. (When competition in one market is weaker than competition in other markets, firms in the less competitive market have more ability to charge prices above cost without losing business. Faced with a tax, those firms may find it more profitable to pass along less than the full amount of the tax—in order to retain more of their business—than to pass along the entire tax. In strongly competitive markets such as the trucking industry, firms do not have the ability to absorb additional costs without becoming unprofitable. As a result, they lack the option of passing along only part of a tax.) In the simulations, railroads pass along between 90 percent and 100 percent of the tax, and trucking companies are assumed to pass along the entire amount of the tax.[34]

Taxes on a Shipment's Weight, Distance, Fuel Use, or a Combination

One set of options would impose taxes on the weight, distance, and/or fuel consumption of individual shipments. Taxing all of those factors simultaneously would cause shippers—and, ultimately, consumers of the shipped goods—to internalize (pay) all of the external costs listed in Table 1. Approaches that were

---

[33] Federal Highway Administration, *Traffic Congestion and Reliability: Linking Solutions to Problems* (report prepared by Cambridge Systematics with Texas Transportation Institute, July 19, 2004), p. ES-7, ops.fhwa.dot.gov/congestion_report_04/congestion_report.pdf (2.6 MB).

[34] In highly competitive industries like trucking, firms all charge about the same price for the same service, profit margins are very small so firms have very little capacity to absorb any tax costs, and thus all of them pass along those costs to their customers. In somewhat less-competitive industries like freight rail, firms can earn a return by competing on price and thus may find it more profitable to absorb some of the tax than to pass all of it along to their customers.

Table 2.
Policy Options
(2014 dollars)

Option	Average Tax Rates (To be added to any existing tax)	
	Truck	**Railcar**
Taxes on a Shipment's Weight, Distance, Fuel Use, or a Combination		
1. Average External-Cost Taxes[a] (Weight-distance tax plus fuel tax)	3.1 cents per ton-mile (2.3¢/ton-mile + $1.50/gal)	0.5 cents per ton-mile (0.3¢/ton-mile + $1.50/gal)
2. VMT Tax Plus Fuel Tax[a]	30 cents per mile + $1.50 per gallon	12 cents per mile + $1.50 per gallon
3. VMT Tax Only	30 cents per mile	12 cents per mile
4. Fuel Tax Only[a]	$1.50 per gallon	$1.50 per gallon
Taxes on Container Shipments		
5. Intermodal Container Tax[b] (Weight-distance tax plus fuel tax)	3.1 cents per ton-mile	0.5 cents per ton-mile
6. Intermodal Container Tax (Distance zones)	$140-$1,597 based on zone[c]	$27-$309 based on zone[c]
7. Intermodal Container Tax (Uniform)	$286 per container	$138 per container
Taxes on Truck Tires		
8. Excise Tax on Truck Tires	1.5 cents per mile equivalent[d]	not applicable

a. In this analysis, the tax on emissions was assessed on a per ton-mile basis (averaging 0.92¢ and 0.24¢ per ton-mile for truck and rail, respectively). Based on average rates of fuel consumption, those rates imply a fuel tax of about $1.50 per gallon for each mode.

b. Drayage portion of rail journey assessed at higher truck rate. For options 6 and 7 (zone tax and uniform tax), rail tax reflects average external costs of drayage portion of journey.

c. For specific zone taxes, see Table 3. [On March 31, 2015, CBO corrected a reference to this note.]

d. Cents-per-mile equivalent cost per truck is based on 18 wheels; 5,000 lbs rated capacity per tire; 530,000 mile tire life (130,000 miles on original treads and 100,000 miles each on four retreads); and trailer tires, drive tires, and steering tires rolling 130k, 340k, and 530k miles, respectively, on new tires (with all remaining miles on retreads).

narrower in scope, such as taxing only distance (vehicle miles traveled) or increasing the diesel-fuel tax to reflect emissions damages, would be less costly to administer than a tax on weight and distance but would not reflect external costs as accurately or as comprehensively.

Average-External-Cost Taxes. The average external cost (AEC) tax is a combination of a weight-distance tax plus a fuel tax. The AEC tax would address all five of the external costs in Table 1: pavement damage, traffic congestion, and accident risk (each addressed by the weight-distance tax) and emissions of PM and NO_x, as well as carbon dioxide (each addressed by the fuel tax). In the simulations, the AEC tax is set at 3.1 cents per ton-mile for trucks and 0.5 cents per ton-mile for rail (after converting the fuel tax into cents per ton-mile based on average fuel efficiencies).

An AEC tax on all truck and rail freight—taking into account cargo weight, distance traveled, and emissions—would cause shippers to pay the average external costs of freight transport. The information required to administer such a tax includes payload weight and distance of every freight shipment. Those data are recorded on the waybill for each shipment and handled in electronic form by private firms like Railinc—a subsidiary of the Association of American Railroads—that process and deliver waybill messages. The federal government does not collect those data. (The freight data in this analysis come from the Commodity Flow Survey.) Even if, as an alternative, cargo weights could be recorded en route, waybills would still be needed for observing distance.[35]

The AEC policy is designed to counteract the average market distortions caused by freight-transport prices that do not reflect external costs.[36] In the future, on-board and remote technologies to monitor payload weights, distances, fuel use, and traffic congestion could support more finely tuned policies, including policies that would vary by location and time of day.

Taxes on Vehicle Miles Traveled. The VMT tax is an alternative to the weight-distance tax that requires less information to administer. It is patterned after several states' highway freight taxes, except that it is also imposed on railcars. In the simulations, the VMT tax reflects the external costs of pavement damage, accident risk, and traffic congestion, not of emissions. For trucks, the VMT tax rate is 30 cents per (laden) mile, versus 12 cents per mile for each railcar. Those rates diverge much less than the underlying, per ton-mile damages—for example, average noncompensated accident damages are an estimated 1.57 cents per ton-mile for trucks, versus 0.18 cents for rail—because a typical truck payload weighs much less than a railcar payload, and thus a truck VMT involves, on average, fewer ton-miles than does a railcar VMT.[37] In the simulations, the VMT tax does not apply to empty-return miles, because the source data do not include unladen miles. However, as noted in the appendix, the estimated external costs of empty returns have been prorated over laden miles. If the data included empty returns, VMT tax rates of 25 cents per mile and 10 cents per mile, for truck and rail, respectively, would generate about the same revenue as the VMT rates used in the simulations.[38]

Relative to the AEC tax, the VMT tax creates incentives for shippers to send their cargo in fewer, heavier shipments because it taxes only distance, not weight. Heavy shipments can do more damage to public roads than to rails—and most rails are privately owned—so those incentives could be socially costly. However, the potential for weight-related damage is limited by maximum weight restrictions on truck cargo. Those restrictions can be exceeded, but only with permission from state authorities; the carrier may be required to use a trailer with additional axles to distribute the load and minimize pavement damage.

Kentucky is the only state that imposes a freight VMT tax, at about 3 cents per truck mile, including empty returns. The truck taxes in New Mexico, New York, and Oregon are weight-distance taxes because they vary by truck weight class and, in some cases, by whether the truck is empty or laden. But within

---

[35] Although there are not enough public highway scales to weigh every freight shipment, the scales could be used to weigh randomly selected shipments in support of a tax based on self-reported weights. Adjustments would be needed for "less-than-truckload" shipping because those payloads gradually diminish as the truck makes deliveries. However, the majority of truck ton-miles occur in the (full) truckload segment.

[36] Market distortions are misallocations of resources, such as when shippers' mode choices and quantities shipped are affected by the absence of external costs from shipping prices.

[37] In sensitivity testing, the rail accident risk is doubled in response to the increased risk posed by crude-oil shipments as demonstrated by several severe accidents involving trains carrying Bakken crude oil.

[38] Based on 19 percent of each mode's total miles being empty returns. See Federal Railroad Administration, *Final Report: Comparative Evaluation of Rail and Truck Fuel Efficiency on Competitive Corridors* (November 19, 2009), Exhibit 4-7, p. 69.

weight classes, those states' taxes are like VMT taxes. Oregon's tax rate for large freight trucks is 16 cents per mile; in New Mexico and New York, the rate is around 5 cents per mile.[39] Those rates apply to empty returns as well.

Taxing all miles gives freight carriers a stronger incentive to minimize their empty returns. But carriers already have every incentive to do so to keep costs low. Thus, simulating a VMT tax only on laden miles would probably yield results similar to those from a simulated tax on all miles, using those lower tax rates.

Taxes on Diesel Fuel. The simulated fuel taxes—which carriers would pay in addition to the current fuel tax—reflect external costs from emissions of PM, NO_x, and CO_2. Table 1 reports estimates of those costs in cents per ton-mile. On average, those costs are the equivalent of about $1.50 per gallon of diesel fuel, based on estimated average fuel efficiency of about 150 ton-miles per gallon for freight trucks and about 475 ton-miles per gallon for trains.[40] Trucks now pay an average of 54.4 cents per gallon in federal and state fuel taxes.[41] Railroads pay only the 0.1¢ per gallon federal tax for the Leaking Underground Storage Tank Trust Fund, and many states waive their taxes on diesel fuel when used in locomotives.[42]

The excise taxes on diesel fuel (and on truck tires, discussed below) would have the lowest administrative costs among the simulated taxes: To implement them requires no information about freight shipments, and their point-of-sale collections are already in place. The trade-off is that fuel taxes target most external costs only indirectly. Fuel taxes do target emissions of carbon dioxide directly, because the carbon content of fuels is known and is not captured by any current technology. But fuel taxes only target other external costs via the correlation between fuel consumption and VMT or other emissions.

Container Taxes

This paper examines three kinds of intermodal container taxes: one based on weight and distance, one on distance only, and a uniform tax that does not depend on either. The taxes target all of the external costs listed in Table 1 and would apply to intermodal freight carried overland by truck or rail. (The three options for a container tax differ considerably in their design. As a result they target the external costs with greater or lesser precision and have varying effects on intermodal transport.) A tax on overland transport of intermodal containers would have an analogous effect on shippers' mode choices to that of the first four policy options: To the extent that the tax was greater for a container shipped by truck than by rail, it would encourage some shippers to switch from truck to rail. Because the tax would apply only to containerized freight, it would create incentives for shippers not to use intermodal transport (or to repackage their imported, containerized freight once it reaches port). But as simulated, the taxes are too small, compared with the cost savings from containerizing, to make repackaging (or avoiding intermodal transport altogether) worthwhile for very many shippers.

---

[39] New York's tax rate on empty trucks is around 3.5 cents per mile. An empty tractor-trailer weighs about 17 tons. A fully-loaded tractor-trailer usually cannot exceed 40 tons including freight. (Without a special permit, interstate highway truck weights are restricted to 80,000 pounds.) See Department of Energy, *2012 Vehicle Technologies Market Report* (March 2014), p. 68, http://cta.ornl.gov/vtmarketreport/index.shtml.

[40] Texas Transportation Institute, *A Modal Comparison of Domestic Freight Transportation Effects on the General Public, 2001-2009* (February 2012), pp.5-6, www.nationalwaterwaysfoundation.org/study/FinalReportTTI.pdf (2.2 MB). Rail estimate applies to locomotives hauling double-stacked containers.

[41] American Petroleum Institute, *State Motor Fuel Taxes* (revised February 12, 2015), www.api.org.

[42] Federal Highway Administration, "Fuel Sales and Taxes: Exemptions," www.fhwa.dot.gov/motorfuel/sales_taxes_exemptions.htm.

Table 3.
Container Zone Taxes
(2014 dollars)

Mode	Distance				
	0–500 Miles	500–1,000 Miles	1,000–2,000 Miles	2,000–3,000 Miles	>3,000 Miles
Truck	140	394	728	1,237	1,597
Rail	27	75	140	239	309

Weight- and Distance-Based Container Tax. The benchmark container-tax option is the AEC tax on weight and distance, but applied only to containers. In the simulations, that tax is set at 3.1 cents per ton-mile for truck transport and 0.5 cents per ton-mile for rail. (See Table 2.) The analysis compares that tax to two other options with lower administrative costs: a distance-based container tax that ignores weight, and a uniform tax that does not depend on distance or weight.

Distance-Based Container Tax. The distance-only container tax is based on a simplified zone structure like those used by some private package couriers: All trips whose distance falls within a given range are assessed the same tax. The zone tax is similar to the VMT tax in that it is based on distance but not weight. The only difference is that the zone tax is based, roughly, on a zone's midpoint distance rather than on actual miles. Thus, all trips of between 1,000 and 2,000 miles, say, are assessed a tax based on a distance of 1,500 miles.[43] Administrators could also define zones by dividing the United States into regions and basing the taxes on the average distance between each pair of regions. Here, for simplicity, zones are defined by travel distance, but the effect is the same. Within each zone, or range of travel distances, there is one unvarying tax for trucks and another for rail. (See Table 3.)

Uniform Tax. The third kind of intermodal container tax is a uniform tax on trips of all distances and all weights, as if the country were a single zone. Compared to the zone tax, a one-size-fits-all uniform tax that was simply based on the external costs for a trip of average distance—around $100 for a container shipped by rail and $500 for a container shipped by truck—would impose very large increases in shipping costs over the shortest distances and much smaller increases over longer distances.[44] However, taking into account that shipping prices seem to reflect a smaller share of external costs as trip distance increases, the uniform taxes for rail and truck in the simulations are $138 and $286, respectively. The ratio of those taxes, at a little more than 1 to 2, is different from the 1 to 8 ratio of the modes' per-ton-mile external costs. The tax on trucked containers is relatively low in this analysis because it is a per-trip tax; trucking

---

[43] In the data, carriers' prices per ton-mile increase more slowly with distance than do the estimated external costs. For that reason, the zone tax cannot be based simply on a mode's external costs at the midpoint distance, because it would not fully cover external costs unless a majority of trips in each zone happened to be shorter than the zone's midpoint distance. The tax takes into account the divergence of carrier rates from external costs so that it has the same average effect on shipping costs as the ASC container tax has, given the data. That adjustment lowers truck taxes in Table 3 by 7 percent and increases rail taxes by 24 percent relative to taxes based simply on each zone's midpoint distance. The adjustment affects the modes differently because of differences in their average trip lengths and rate structures in the data.

[44] With maximum-weight restrictions on shipping containers that allow for safe handling, there is relatively little variation in intermodal shipping weights. Thus, although the uniform fees do not take weight into account, they are nowhere near as burdensome on smaller payloads as they are on shorter-distance trips.

dominates short-haul markets, so that mode's higher total external costs can be allocated over many more trips. As with the zone tax, the revenue from the uniform tax would fully cover each mode's baseline external costs, and the tax would have the same average effect on shipping costs. For context, the federal Harbor Maintenance Tax averaged about $109 per imported 40-foot container in 2012.[45] As previously noted, certain ports also charge fees ranging from $20 to more than $120 for each container.

Truck Tire Tax

New truck tires are taxed at 0.945 cents for every pound of rated weight-bearing capacity over 3,500 pounds. Policymakers have recently considered a tenth-of-a-cent increase in the tax on new truck tires, to 1.045 cents.[46] (There is no tax on retreaded truck tires.) The option examined in this section would increase the tax on new truck tires by 0.5 cents—to 1.445 cents—and would apply the tax to retreads as well. Even with that much larger tax on truck tires, the tax would still reflect only a small share of the highway-related external costs from freight trucks (that is, pavement damage, traffic congestion, and accident risk).

On average, if truck tires last 530,000 miles (one expert's estimate), including their retread miles, the incremental cost of this option's increase in the tire tax—including the full 1.445-cent increase on retreads—would be around 1.5 cents per mile (for an 18-wheel truck) compared with costs under current policy.[47] That increase would amount to $8,135 per truck every 530,000 miles: $75 more per new tire plus $217.50 per retread. For the median truck payload of about 16 tons, the tire-tax increase translates into a median tax rate of less than 0.1 cent per ton-mile. For comparison, in the simulations the AEC tax rate on truck freight is 3.1 cents per ton-mile.

That tire tax would represent a 50 percent increase over the current tax on new tires and an entirely new levy on retreads. Because tire wear is imperfectly correlated with payload weight, the new tire tax (like the VMT tax) would not be well-suited to internalizing weight-related external costs (such as pavement damage). However, extending the tax to retreaded tires might better capture freight trucks' external highway costs, because most "truck tire miles" are probably retread miles. (Truck tires are designed to be retreaded multiple times.) Applying the tax only to new tires would increase carriers' incentives to rely on retreaded tires. Some analysts assert that retreads are less safe than new tires, although others contend that retreads and new tires are equally safe.[48] But imposing a larger tax increase on retreaded tires than on

[45] Federal Maritime Commission, *Study of U.S. Inland Containerized Cargo Moving Through Canadian and Mexican Seaports* (July 2012), pp. 41 and 55, www.fmc.gov/assets/1/News/Study_of_US_Inland_Containerized_Cargo_Moving_Through_Canadian_and_Mexican_Seaports_Final.pdf (2.2 MB).

[46] Senate Committee on Finance, *Infrastructure, Energy, and Natural Resources* (April 25, 2013), www.finance.senate.gov/issue/?id=8b4a11ec-b93f-43bd-8f72-fbc4f4768989.

[47] That estimate is based on the following parameters: 5,000 pounds rated capacity per tire, meaning 1,500 pounds of *taxed* capacity net of 3,500 pounds (see, for example, www.bridgestonetrucktires.com/us_eng/real/magazines/ra_v15i1/ra_techspk.asp); 530,000 mile tire life (nominal truck-tire life is 600,000 to 700,000 miles based on manufacturer warranties (for instance, Michelin); and 130,000 miles on original treads and 100,000 miles each on four retreads (personal communication with Knight Transportation). For every 530,000 miles of driving, trailer tires, drive tires, and steering tires roll 130,000, 340,000, and 530,000 miles, respectively, on new tires; all remaining miles are on retreads. Those parameters imply, for instance, that truckers never use retreads as steering tires and that most trailer miles are on retreads.

[48] See, for instance, Washington State Department of Transportation, *Retreaded Tire Use and Safety: Synthesis* (September 3, 2009), www.wsdot.wa.gov/nr/rdonlyres/66366b14-f8b2-43a2-8495-16ce599469fa/0/retreadtiresynthesis9309.pdf (708 KB).

new tires, as in the simulation, could discourage retreading to the point where trucking companies would discard old tires well before the end of their service life.

Effects of Policy Options

The findings presented here are the averaged results from 1,000 runs of the simulation model. For each run, new values were selected for the model's random parameters: rates charged by truck and rail carriers; mode-choice elasticities (shippers' price sensitivities); freight lift costs and drayage trip lengths; rail route circuity (additional miles of travel when shipping by rail versus truck); the tax pass-through rate (the share of the tax that the shippers pay); average payload sizes; and mode fuel efficiencies. The randomness of the parameters, as described in the appendix, reflects uncertainty in their estimated values.

The tax rates used in the simulations are based on the averages of the ranges of unpriced external costs. Separately, actual external-cost values are selected for each run from the distributions around those averages. The selected values represent one possibility for the "true" (unobserved) costs; those values represent the difference between each tax rate and its associated external cost. That difference reflects uncertainty about the actual external costs per ton-mile in typical conditions.

Theoretically, if shippers and consumers of shipped products paid no other taxes, then setting the taxes equal to external costs would be economically efficient, because the external costs of shipping would be fully incorporated in the prices of shipments. In practice, however, taxes on shipments would compound the costs associated with current taxes on individual and corporate income, so the incremental cost to the economy from those freight taxes would be higher than the actual tax rates would suggest. If the revenues from the freight taxes were used in ways that did not offset that compounding effect—for example, if they were distributed to all U.S. residents on an equal lump-sum basis—the economically efficient tax rates would probably be lower than the external costs. Alternatively, to the extent that lawmakers used the tax revenues in ways that offset the taxes' negative effects on real (inflation-adjusted) wages, investment, and output, the efficient rates of the taxes would be closer to—or perhaps even greater than—the external costs.[49]

Shippers' responses to the taxes—some shippers would switch to a less-preferred transport mode for some deliveries—would reduce external costs. In doing so, they would incur costs because their clients would generally not be willing to pay as much for that less-preferred service, perhaps because of longer or less-convenient delivery times. (Those costs would ultimately be borne by consumers.) Shippers who switched from truck to rail would generally do so because their costs of switching would be lower than the taxes they would incur by not switching modes.

If the taxes on truck and rail in fact equaled actual external costs, then the social gains would exceed consumers' losses, on average. If the taxes were below the actual external costs, then too little mode-switching would occur—meaning not only that the social gains would exceed consumers' losses, but that if the taxes were raised toward the external costs, then the incremental social gains from that adjustment would also exceed consumers' incremental losses, on average. If the taxes were above the actual external costs, then too much mode-switching would occur. The taxes would need to be far above the actual external costs, though, for the total losses by consumers to more than offset the total social gains.

Under policies that taxed external costs, freight carriers would probably respond in additional ways that are not incorporated in the simulations. For example, carriers might try to reduce their external costs by

---

[49]For additional discussion of how to determine the tax rate that best balances benefits and costs when external costs are involved, see Congressional Budget Office, *Effects of a Carbon Tax on the Economy and the Environment* (May 2013), pp. 17–18, www.cbo.gov/publication/44223.

adopting cleaner technologies to reduce emissions; adding tankers or railcars with increased resistance to spills; developing new accident-avoidance technologies and operator-training methods; or distributing loads over more truck axles to reduce pavement damage. Because such responses would probably occur eventually if external costs were taxed, the results described below should be considered medium-run responses that would take some time to develop and that would eventually be neutralized, at least in part, by carriers' technology adoptions and other strategic responses.

Taxes on a Shipment's Weight, Distance, Fuel Use, or a Combination

Imposing taxes that reflected the external costs of freight transport (though inevitably with some error) would require knowing the weight, distance, and mode of transport of each shipment, because the external costs of freight transport depend on those factors. If the costs to administer a tax based on both weight and distance would be an obstacle to its adoption (pending the development or adoption of new information technologies), the VMT tax on shipping distance only—not weight—is an alternative that would impose lower administrative costs, albeit an alternative that would not reflect external costs as accurately as a weight-distance tax. A tax on fuel consumption only would be still less costly to administer; in this scenario, it would reflect solely the cost of unpriced emissions.[50]

Average-External-Cost Taxes. In the simulations, the AEC tax—a tax on the weight and distance of a shipment along with a tax on fuel use—raised truck shipping prices by an average of about 19 percent and rail prices by about 12 percent, taking into account shippers' responses to the taxes. (See the first column of Table 4.) In response to the increase in shipping costs, total freight shipping declined only slightly—by 0.8 percent—because, in most cases, shipping costs are a small fraction of a commodity's price, and the demand for freight transport is derived from demand for those shipped commodities. In the simulation data, shipping costs average around 4 percent of total costs (see Table A-6 for transport cost shares by type of freight). Thus, the increase in average shipping costs from the AEC tax represented only about 0.6 percent of the average price of shipped goods.

The AEC tax would have a much greater effect on shippers' mode choices than it would on total shipping. The simulated AEC tax caused some shippers to shift some of their business away from trucking (the costs to ship by truck were most affected by the tax) and toward rail. The size of the effect varied by commodity and route, depending on the increase in the cost to ship by truck relative to rail. On average, the simulated AEC tax would have caused trucking costs to rise relative to rail in 2007 by approximately 6 percent, or (1.19/1.12), causing about 4 percent of truck ton-miles to shift to rail. (Including the slight market contraction, or reduction in tons shipped, truck ton-miles declined by nearly 5 percent.) In tons, the shift would have been only 0.6 percent, indicating that most of the shift occurred on long-haul routes. Very little mode-shifting occurred on shorter routes, where trucks have a particular competitive advantage over rail (because of lower costs and faster service on those routes).

Rail ton-miles in 2007 would have increased by 3.5 percent.[51] (The increase would have been 5 percent excluding Wyoming coal, which accounts for many ton-miles and is shipped almost exclusively by rail.) That increase implies that the AEC tax would probably have eliminated around 3.2 million highway truck trips annually (based on typical truck payloads) and increased the number of railcar trips by around 0.8

---

[50] To tax rail diesel fuel at a different rate from truck diesel fuel would not require any new infrastructure to separate the two fuel supplies, because they are already kept separate and taxed at different rates.

[51] The analysis does not consider the amount of time the nation's freight-rail network might need to develop adequate capacity to absorb such an increase in demand. Robust growth in the U.S. economy before 2008 created concerns about rail's "absorptive capacity." See Congressional Budget Office, *Freight Rail Transportation: Long-Term Issues* (January 2006), www.cbo.gov/publication/17597. Alternatively, a tax increase could be phased in over time, giving the freight rail and trucking industries time to adjust.

Table 4.
Effects of Policy Options on Transport in 2007 (If policy had been in effect before that year)

Policies Concerning:	Truck and Rail Transport				Container Freight *			Trucks Only
Policy: / OUTCOME	Weight/Distance & Fuel Taxes (Avg External Costing)	VMT & Fuel Taxes	VMT Tax Only	Fuel Tax Only	Avg External Costing Container Tax	Uniform Container Tax	Zone Distance Container Tax	Tire Tax
Avg. Shipping-Cost Increase, Rail (%)	12.1	15.9	10.1	5.9	10.5	10.5	10.5	0.1
Avg. Shipping-Cost Increase, Truck (%)	18.9	19.3	12.6	6.6	16.5	16.5	16.5	0.9
Market Contraction								
Reduction, total tons shipped (%)	-0.8	-0.7	-0.5	-0.3	-0.04	-0.2	-0.1	-0.03
Mode Choice (pct effects)								
Reduction, ton-miles, truck (%)	-4.5	-4.8	-4.4	-1.1	-1.1	-0.9	-1.4	-0.7
Increase, ton-miles, rail (%)	3.5	4.0	4.2	0.7	1.1	0.7	1.3	0.7
Shift, ton-miles: truck to RR (%)	3.6	3.9	3.8	0.8	1.0	0.7	1.2	0.6
Shift, tonnage: truck to RR (%)	0.6	0.6	0.5	0.1	0.1	0.2	0.2	0.1
Mode Choice (level effects)								
Net shift, ton-mi, truck to RR (bn)	70	75	74	16	19	13	23	12
Reduction, truck trips (000)	-3,193	-3,348	-2,671	-895	-724	-2,122	-1,431	-351
Increase, rail-car trips (000)	794	881	817	162	420	716	684	135

Notes: 1,000 iterations per policy; standard errors not reported.
* = Cost increases for container policies apply only to intermodal freight.

million. (For average payloads by commodity, see Table A-8.) The increase in railcar trips would have been smaller because one railcar can haul multiple truckloads of freight.

Fuel consumption for freight transport would have declined by almost 3 percent, or by roughly 670 million gallons per year. Most of the savings would have stemmed from rail's substantially better fuel efficiency; some savings would have come from the slight reduction in overall freight shipping. The projected annual revenue from the tax would have been $68 billion in 2007. In competitive markets, the tax would have been paid by shippers, not the truck and rail carriers.[52]

The tax payments cover the costs of the pavement damage, traffic congestion, accidents, and emissions that would still occur with the AEC tax in place. In total, the AEC tax would have also reduced annual external costs by around $2.3 billion through mode shifts and market contraction. (See Table 5.) The $2.3 billion in external costs would have been avoided by sending slightly less freight and by shifting some

---

[52] Net external costs could be further affected by the uses that revenue were put to, such as financing infrastructure investments or reducing other, distortionary taxes. This paper does not analyze the implications of revenue use.

Table 5.
Effects of Policy Options on External Costs, Fuel Use, and Revenues in 2007 (If policy had been in effect before that year)

Policies Concerning:	Truck and Rail Transport				Container Freight			Trucks Only
Policy: OUTCOME	Weight/Distance & Fuel Taxes (Avg External Costing)	VMT & Fuel Taxes	VMT Tax Only	Fuel Tax Only	Avg External Costing Container Tax	Uniform Container Tax	Zone Distance Container Tax	Tire Tax
Percentage Effects								
Change, social costs (%)	-3.3	-3.4	-3.1	-0.9	-0.8	-0.6	-1.0	-0.5
Fuel savings (%)	2.9	3.0	2.7	0.8	0.7	0.6	0.8	0.4
Level Effects								
Fuel savings (millions of gal.)	669	696	623	176	161	127	192	91
Chng, external costs (billions of 2014 $)	-2.3	-2.4	-2.1	-0.6	-0.6	-0.4	-0.7	-0.3
Tax revenue (billions of 2014 $)	68	70	43	26	13	28	16	4

Note: 1,000 iterations per policy; standard errors not reported.

business from truck to rail in response to the tax. The incentives created by the tax were designed so that the private value of the forgone transport, and of truck transport relative to rail for the freight that was shifted, would have been less than the external costs those activities had been imposing.

The effects of the simulated AEC tax would have differed somewhat by type of freight service, because of differences in the baseline rates that carriers charge for different types of freight, in the propensities of shippers to switch modes, and in the sensitivity of customers to the prices of the final goods. (See Table 6.) Rail ton-miles would have increased for every type of freight except bulk commodities, for which the simulated AEC tax caused rail shipping costs to increase relatively more (because bulk payloads are often heavy and rail rates per ton-mile are relatively low) than for other kinds of freight. That relatively large increase in rail rates for bulk commodities, combined with bulk-commodity shippers' low propensities to shift modes and rail's relatively large share of bulk freight ton-miles, meant that rail gained very little new bulk-freight business from trucking. According to the tax simulation, rail would have lost slightly more bulk freight business through market contraction than it would have gained from mode shifts.

By contrast, rail intermodal transport would have gained the most new business when the AEC tax was applied, an 11 percent increase in railcar trips. Rail rates tend to be higher for intermodal transport than for other types of freight transport, so the percentage increase in rail intermodal rates from the tax would have been smaller. As a result, the relative increase in truck rates would have been larger, which, in combination with higher mode-choice elasticities for the finished goods that tend to be shipped in intermodal containers, would make for a larger shift of that containerized freight toward rail (see Table A-5). Because of rail's relatively smaller share of intermodal freight ton-miles—according to the data—any given shift from trucking also would have represented a larger percentage increase in rail business. (See Table A-1). Rail intermodal transport would have had less market contraction as a result of the tax,

Table 6.
Effects of Policy Options on Mode Choice by Type of Freight in 2007 (If policy had been in effect before that year)

Policies Concerning:	Truck and Rail Transport				Container Freight			Trucks Only
Policy: **OUTCOME**	Weight/Distance & Fuel Taxes (Full External Costing)	VMT & Fuel Taxes	VMT Tax Only	Fuel Tax Only	Avg External Costing Container Tax	Uniform Container Tax	Zone Distance Container Tax	Tire Tax
Carload/Truckload freight								
% Reduction, truck trips	-1.2	-1.2	-1.0	-0.3	0	0	0	-0.1
% Increase, railcar trips	8.4	7.7	7.2	1.9	0	0	0	1.1
Bulk freight								
% Reduction, truck trips	-1.7	-1.6	-1.1	-0.6	0	0	0	-0.1
% Increase, railcar trips	-0.1	0	0.2	-0.1	0	0	0	0.1
Intermodal freight								
% Reduction, truck trips	-1.8	-2.2	-1.8	-0.4	-1.8	-5.4	-3.6	-0.3
% Increase, railcar trips	11.3	14.5	13.3	2.1	11.3	19.3	18.4	2.3
Automobile transport								
% Reduction, truck trips	-1.7	-1.8	-1.3	-0.6	0	0	0	-0.1
% Increase, railcar trips	3.6	2.9	2.2	1.1	0	0	0	0.4

Note: 1,000 iterations per policy; standard errors not reported.

because intermodal shipping costs tend to be only a small share of the goods' prices, especially for the many high-value finished goods that would have been shipped intermodally.

VMT Taxes and Fuel Taxes. Compared with the AEC tax, the VMT tax—which does not use information about shipping weight—trades off potentially smaller social gains for lower administrative costs. By imposing the same per-mile tax rates on all shipments regardless of weight, the VMT tax would, in effect, cause lighter freight shipments to subsidize some of the external costs of heavy freight. As a result, according to the VMT tax simulations, more lightweight freight—and less heavy freight—would have switched to rail in 2007 than would have been the case with a weight-distance tax. (The simulated AEC tax includes both a weight-distance tax and a fuel tax.) However, that effect would not have been very big. The difference between light and heavy shipments for trucks is much less than for rail because truck payload tonnages vary much less than railcar payloads. As a result, for trucked freight the cost to shippers of a VMT tax would have been similar to what a weight-distance tax would have cost. (See Table A-8 for average payloads by commodity and mode.)

The VMT tax and fuel tax would have induced an additional five billion ton-miles to shift from truck to rail (75 billion ton-miles rather than 70 billion under the AEC tax). In addition, about 3.3 million annual truck trips would have been eliminated rather than 3.2 million, and an additional 27 million gallons of fuel would have been saved per year (4 percent more than under the AEC tax). Among the simulated policies, the AEC tax would have presented shippers with the best approximation of their actual external costs, so the additional impacts of the combined VMT and fuel taxes would have produced smaller social gains than the AEC tax would have (ignoring savings in administrative costs). According to the simulations, the combination of a VMT tax and a fuel tax would have raised rail shipping costs by 16 percent (versus 12 percent with the AEC policy), and truck shipping costs would have been slightly higher. The combined VMT and fuel taxes would also have raised $70 billion from shippers in 2007, $2 billion more than the AEC tax would have raised.

If the administrative cost savings of the VMT tax would have exceeded $2 billion per year, then the net social gains from a VMT tax combined with a fuel tax could have been greater than those from the AEC tax. But those savings would have to have been enough greater than $2 billion to compensate for the social losses associated with the 5 billion additional ton-miles that would have switched from truck to rail because the VMT tax ignores shipping weight. The losses from that additional mode-switching may have been small, however, because they would involve shippers who would have been nearly indifferent between truck and rail.[53]

The effect of the VMT tax on transport would have been similar to the effect of the VMT tax combined with the fuel tax. According to the simulations, the VMT tax alone would have induced a net shift of 74 billion ton-miles from truck to rail (versus 75 billion ton-miles when combined with a fuel tax). The incremental effect of the fuel tax would have been very small in that case, because the fuel tax would have had only modestly different effects on rail shipping costs, given the VMT tax, than it would have had on the costs to ship by truck, despite rail's greater fuel efficiency and lower fuel-tax rate. (That outcome, in turn, is partly because rail pays very little in fuel taxes.) By itself, however, the fuel tax would have induced a shift of 16 billion ton-miles from truck to rail.

The one way in which the two policies' effects do add up to the effect they would have had if both were imposed is in the amount of revenue generated. That is because even though the incremental effect of the fuel tax on shippers' behavior would have been small when both taxes were combined, shippers would still have paid both taxes. When imposed together, the taxes would have generated around $70 billion in annual federal revenue in 2007, compared with around $43 billion from the VMT tax alone and $26 billion from the increase in the federal fuel tax. (For comparison, in 2014 the highway account of the Highway Trust Fund was credited with around $34 billion in fuel-tax and other revenue plus interest, CBO has estimated. About $20 billion of that amount was from taxes paid by freight trucking companies, primarily the federal tax on diesel fuel.)

Container Taxes

In the simulations, the AEC container tax (based on weight, distance, and fuel consumption) would have increased average shipping costs less than the AEC tax on all freight did. Costs would have increased by about 10 percent and 16 percent for intermodal rail and truck transport in 2007, respectively, because carriers' intermodal rates were slightly higher, in the data, than the average for all freight. (See Table A-4.) The container taxes would have caused comparatively little market contraction—just a 0.04 percent reduction in tons shipped versus 0.8 percent for the AEC tax on all freight. Based just on the share of freight tonnage in the intermodal category—around 10 percent of total tons shipped, according to the data used in the simulation model—the container tax might have been expected to have one-tenth the effect of the AEC tax, or a contraction of 0.08 percent. The contraction would have been only half as great because intermodal freight often consists of finished goods (such as furniture, electronics, machinery, and textiles)

---

[53] Because most railcar payloads average either below 30 tons or above 70 tons (see Table A-8), the excessive mode-shifting could be limited by imposing a higher VMT tax rate on railcars that could accommodate the heavier payloads.

with relatively high value-to-weight ratios, and thus shipping costs for such freight are often a smaller share of final prices.

The AEC container tax would have resulted in more mode-switching than the same tax applied to all freight, according to the simulations: Even though container freight accounted for only 14 percent of total ton-miles in the data, it accounted for nearly 30 percent of the ton-miles that would have switched from truck to rail. If a container tax had been implemented, 19 billion ton-miles of intermodal freight transport would have switched from truck to rail, versus 70 billion ton-miles from the AEC tax on all freight.

The uniform and zone container taxes would both have had lower administrative costs than the AEC tax because they require less information. But policymakers would have to weigh those savings against the additional costs of those policies: Compared with the AEC tax, which more accurately reflects external costs, the uniform and zone taxes would have caused more market exit, much greater reductions in truck trips, and more tax revenue to be collected per dollar of reduction in external costs. Applied to trips of all distances, the uniform tax would have shifted 30 percent fewer truck ton-miles than the AEC tax on containers and eliminated almost three times as many truck trips. Although the uniform tax on trucked containers, as simulated, was only about double the rail tax (whereas the external costs to ship by truck are about eight times higher than by rail), that uniform tax inevitably would have been burdensome on shorter truck trips, for which it represented a much larger increase in shipping costs than it did for longer trips. Evidence for that can be seen in the much greater effect that the uniform tax would have had on truck trips than on truck ton-miles, indicating that the uniform tax would have eliminated more short truck trips than long trips. The uniform tax also would have caused more than six times as much tonnage to exit from transport markets than the AEC container tax would have (0.25 percent versus 0.04 percent) while collecting more than twice as much tax revenue from shippers ($28 billion versus $13 billion) in 2007. Finally, in shifting fewer ton-miles from truck to rail, the uniform container tax would have reduced fuel use by only 127 million gallons per year, versus 161 million gallons for the AEC container tax.

The zone-tax simulation produced results much more similar to those of the AEC container tax, although the zone tax still would have greatly affected shorter trips within each zone. (It would have eliminated twice as many truck trips as the AEC tax did, while also shifting an additional 20 percent more ton-miles to rail.) Otherwise, the fuel savings and revenue from the zone tax would have been more like those from the AEC container tax than from the uniform tax. That result shows that the use of a little more information (than that required by the uniform tax policy) in order to define separate tax rates for each zone would have substantially improved upon the performance of the uniform tax policy.[54]

Truck Tire Tax
As simulated, the tire tax would have increased truck shipping costs by less than 1 percent in 2007—just one-twentieth the effect on shipping costs that the AEC tax on all freight had. But it would have induced a shift from truck to rail that was proportionally three times greater than the shift from the AEC tax. According to the simulations, the tire tax would have shifted 12 billion ton-miles to rail, which is more than one-sixth the size of the shift that the AEC tax would have induced (70 billion ton-miles). That proportionally greater shift would have arisen because the tire tax would have directly affected only truck freight. (It would have indirectly affected rail through truck drayage.) The tire tax would have, in effect, primarily targeted the external cost of pavement damage; but at the equivalent of 0.1 cent per ton-mile, that tire tax would have covered only a fraction of the cost of the estimated damage. Based on the simulations, such a tax would have generated $4 billion in revenue (in 2014 dollars).

---

[54] The simulations do not estimate administrative cost savings or any increase in external costs from shippers who "decontainerize" their cargo to avoid the container fee. The latter effect is probably very small because the fee is unlikely to exceed the cost savings of containerization.

Sensitivity Analyses

Those simulation results depend on a range of parameter values. Many of the values are based on careful measurement, but others are less well-understood and therefore more uncertain. True values are not known with certainty even for carefully measured parameters and could lie outside the range used in the simulations. To determine the sensitivity of the results to particular values, the benchmark average-external-cost tax policy was resimulated while systematically varying key parameters. The main finding of that exercise is that the overall results of the policy simulations are relatively insensitive, even to large changes in parameter values.

The model's various parameters were altered individually to see how those changes would affect the main results. (See Table 7 for the average effects over 1,000 simulations.) The "likely range" of values shows how the model's predictions varied when the default values were used for all of the parameters: The range is constructed so that it contains the central two-thirds of the outcomes predicted over 1,000 simulations. That range is centered on the median prediction. In addition, findings from the six sensitivity tests on the most influential parameters are described below. Tests on other parameters are also briefly noted.

This sensitivity analysis only involves uncertainty about the key parameters in the model as applied to data on freight transport observed for 2007. If the model was adapted to predict future effects, then uncertainty about freight transport volumes and other aspects of the data would amplify the uncertainty reflected in this sensitivity analysis. Partly for that reason, the likely ranges for effects (such as the impact on revenues) would be much larger if projected for a future year.

External Costs. External costs' true values are not known with certainty, because the estimates on which the simulated taxes are based cover a range of possible values (see Table 1). Although the taxes remain constant throughout the simulations (they are set to the average of the estimates), in each run of the model new values for the external costs are drawn at random from their estimated ranges. Those values represent one possibility for the external costs' true values. Although policymakers would not know the true values, those possibly true values can be used in the simulations to estimate the expected difference between any of the taxes and the true underlying value of the external costs it targets.

For the AEC tax, in two-thirds of 1,000 repeated simulations the difference between the true external costs and the tax rate was between 4 percent and 28 percent for the truck tax and between 3 percent and 27 percent for the rail tax. (See first two rows of Table 7.) The average difference was around 16 percent. Based on the estimated range, the AEC tax on trucked freight can be expected to differ from the true, unobserved external costs by about half a cent per ton-mile, given that the tax rate is 3.1 cents per ton-mile; for the AEC rail tax, the expected difference is about 0.08 cents per ton-mile, given that the rail tax rate is 0.5 cents per ton-mile. (The AEC tax, like the other simulated policies, is based on multiple external costs; measurement error in the estimated value of one external cost may be balanced by error in the opposite direction for another external cost, because those costs were estimated independently.)

The difference between the tax and the external costs can be positive or negative. That is, the tax may have been set too high or too low. Those differences cannot be eliminated because policymakers cannot know what the true external costs are, only their estimated ranges. But by using the simulations to estimate the likely sizes of the discrepancies, the expected economic costs of the taxes can be determined. If a tax is set too high, it would save additional fuel, prevent more accidents, preserve more pavement from damage, and reduce emissions and congestion to a greater extent than would a tax that precisely equaled external costs. But a tax that is set too high would also induce a greater shift from truck to rail and a greater reduction in total freight transport. And because the tax would exceed the external costs, the economic costs of those effects would exceed the social value of the additional fuel savings and other benefits. Alternatively, if a tax is set too low, freight transport will consume too much fuel and damage too much pavement, for example, in the sense that the benefits of saving more fuel and preserving more pavement would exceed the costs (from slightly raising the tax) of additional mode-shifting and market exit.

Sensitivity Test 1: Double the Railroad Accident Risk. The sensitivity of the model's predictions to the parameter pertaining to rail's accident risk was analyzed separately from the other parameters. The estimated range of rail's accident risk used in the simulations—0.11 cents to 0.25 cents per ton-mile—predates the rise in rail transport of crude oil from the Bakken formation. The number of oil shipments by rail has increased dramatically in recent years, and several derailments have resulted in spills, fires, and deaths. This sensitivity test checks how well the model's predictions would hold up if rail's true accident risk doubled, so that it ranged from 0.22 cents to 0.5 cents per ton-mile. If rail shippers were taxed at a higher rate consistent with doubling the estimated risk of accidents, fewer truck shipments would be diverted to rail in response to the tax.

Test 1 shows that a higher AEC tax shifted about 60 percent fewer ton-miles from truck to rail—2.1 percent rather than 3.6 percent under the default values; fuel savings declined by a similar amount. (See Table 7, Test 1.) As with all of the results, the sensitivity tests are based on 1,000 iterations.

Sensitivity Test 2: Ignore Drayage and Lift Costs. Rail delivery of bulk freight and automobiles does not require either drayage or lifting in the simulations. In the model, drayage and lift costs—as described in the appendix—apply to intermodal and carload freight only. Sensitivity testing considered the following variations on those costs: (1) they are zero; (2) there is a short dray from origin to railhead; and (3) drayage and lift costs apply only to intermodal freight, not carload. The first of those tests had the greatest effect (see Table 7, Test 2). In simulations with no drayage or lift costs, the AEC tax had a smaller effect on rail shipping costs because rail shippers now do not face the (higher) truck tax rate on the drayage portion of a rail journey. By contrast, truck shipping costs increased more because the lift charges had contributed to baseline shipping costs (the denominator in the calculation of the tax effect on truck costs) and were not subject to the AEC tax (in the numerator in that calculation).

With a larger increase in truck costs and a smaller increase in rail costs under this test case, the model predicted the following effects: a larger shift toward rail—4.1 percent of truck ton-miles rather than 3.6 percent under the model's default assumptions about drayage and lift costs; somewhat more market contraction; and thus a greater reduction in external costs. Only carload and intermodal freight were affected.

Sensitivity Tests 3 and 4: Use Alternate Mode-Choice Elasticities. To represent mode-choice elasticities, the simulation model could rely on either of several independent sets of estimates from the published literature. The two sets of elasticity estimates best suited to the analysis differ markedly. The elasticities used in the simulation model are much more variable, with values ranging from approximately 0 to 7. (Many of the values cluster around 0.5 for bulk freight or 4 for finished goods.) The other set of elasticities ranges from 0.9 to 1.6. The basis for choosing the first set is twofold. First, individual shippers of bulk freight—especially of large quantities of coal, cereal grains, or gravel—are likely to be relatively dependent on one transport mode and thus not able to switch easily. Second, shippers of intermodal freight—which tends to include more finished goods—can switch transport modes relatively easily because shipping containers are designed for that purpose.

With the alternative mode-choice elasticities, much more bulk freight and automotive freight shifts to rail (because the alternate elasticities are bigger for those types of freight) and much less intermodal and carload freight shifts to rail (because the alternate elasticities are smaller). (See Table 7, Test 3.) Because of rail's relatively smaller market shares in intermodal and carload freight than in bulk freight, the latter effect dominates. As a result, the predicted shift toward rail and the reduction in external costs are both smaller and now lie slightly outside the likely range under the model's default assumptions.

A second sensitivity test considers the influence of the very high mode-switching propensities on finished goods in the model's default elasticities. In that test, all of the mode-choice elasticities greater than 1 were reassigned values closer to 1. Larger values were compressed more than smaller values so that instead of ranging from 1 to 7 they ranged from 1 to 2.5. That compression substantially reduced the predicted shift from truck to rail and thus the total fuel savings and the total reduction in external costs from the AEC tax. But those results remain consistent with the overall conclusions of the analysis. (See Table 7, Test 4.)

Sensitivity Tests 5 and 6: Raise and Lower Truck Shipping Rates. Truck shipping rates (prices) are proprietary and not easily acquired. The truck rates in the simulation model reflect the average truck revenue per ton-mile for "general freight common carriers" estimated by the Bureau of Transportation Statistics.[55] That estimate, however, contains no information about how truck rates vary across commodities or routes. [56] That information comes instead from estimates used in FHWA's "Intermodal Transportation and Inventory Costing" (ITIC) model, which vary by commodity and distance.[57] (See Table A-4.)

Because of that indirect provenance, the rates are subjected here to sensitivity testing. If truck rates are actually higher than those estimates, then true policy effects will be lower than the model predicts: Shippers would be placing a higher value on trucking services, any given tax would represent a smaller increase in price, and shippers would be less likely to switch modes. Likewise, if true truck shipping rates are lower than estimated, then the policy effects would be greater than the model predicts.

To test the model's sensitivity to truck rates, all of the rates were raised, and separately lowered, by 5 percent. If truck rates were 5 percent higher, 3.2 percent of trucked ton-miles would shift to rail (versus 3.6 percent with the default truck rates) and slightly fewer truck trips would be eliminated, around 3.0 million rather than 3.2 million. Reducing truck rates by 5 percent from their default level had effects of about the same magnitude but in the opposite direction. All effects with altered truck rates were within or just slightly outside the model's 67 percent prediction interval for the default rates. (See Table 7, Tests 5 and 6.)

Additional Sensitivity Tests

The sensitivity analysis also included changes to several other sets of parameters. The effects in those sensitivity tests were secondary to those in the primary analysis, so they are briefly described below but are not tabulated.

Transport Cost Shares. The model's transport cost shares, although carefully estimated, are based on data from 1997. (See Table A-6.) Since then, fuel prices have increased substantially, which would tend to boost transport costs as a share of total production costs. But because labor costs have also risen over time, albeit not as much, the effect of rising fuel prices on the importance of transport costs has not been as great as it otherwise would have been. Innovations in logistics management, greater fuel efficiency, and stiffer competition in freight transport also would have helped neutralize the effects of rising fuel

---

[55] Bureau of Transportation Statistics, "National Transportation Statistics," Table 3-21, www.rita.dot.gov/bts/sites/rita.dot.gov.bts/files/publications/national_transportation_statistics/html/table_03_21.html_mfd.

[56] The *rail* rates used in the analysis are based on averages (produced by the Surface Transportation Board) that vary by service type and distance.

[57] For information about the ITIC model, see www.fhwa.dot.gov/policy/otps/061012/iticst_info.htm. The model's truck rate data include costs per mile and payload capacities for 18-wheel tractor-trailers. Because trucks are not usually loaded to full capacity, average rates per ton-mile can be estimated as the ratio of costs per mile to average payload when prices equal costs (as in a competitive industry).

costs. Indeed, total logistics costs, a broader measure that includes transportation costs, has declined slightly since 1997 as a share of gross domestic product.[58] Thus, the 1997 data on transport cost shares are likely still to be reasonably accurate.

To represent statistical uncertainty in those estimates and uncertainty from the passage of time, the simulation model allows current cost shares to be as much as 5 percent higher or 5 percent lower than those estimated in 1997. But because the dampening influence of those mitigating factors has not been measured and because average fuel prices are nearly four times higher than they were in 1997, this sensitivity test considered how the results would differ if transport cost shares increased by 50 percent. In that case, the shares would average around 6 percent, and any increase in transport costs—as from a tax on freight transport—would have a greater effect on product prices than the model currently predicts and cause a bigger contraction in freight transport. But the test found that even if transport cost shares have increased by 50 percent, the effect of the AEC tax would only be reduced by about half a percent, with differences not apparent when results are rounded to tenths (as they are in Table 7).[59]

Market-Specific Adjustments to Mode-Choice Elasticities. In some markets—for reasons of geography, infrastructure, or quantities shipped—shippers may show a stronger preference for one transport mode than they do nationally. In the analysis, those markets were identified by a statistical analysis of mode choice as a function of type of freight, payload value-to-weight ratio, distance, and quoted shipping rates, with individual market effects. Estimating those relationships via a logistic regression model identified a relatively small number of markets in which shippers strongly prefer one mode over the other. In those markets, shippers would be less likely to switch modes in response to a tax than they would in the average market. Mode-choice elasticities in those markets are smaller than in typical markets. The simulation model does not take those lower elasticities into account so, for sensitivity-testing purposes, the mode-choice elasticities in those markets were greatly reduced.[60] (The adjustments were made judgmentally because market-specific elasticity estimates are not available.) Because the adjustments affected only a few markets, they had very little effect on the model's predictions and the test results are not reported.

---

[58] In 1997, the share was more than 10 percent, a level it has not exceeded since 2000. In most years since then the share has been below 9 percent. See International Transport Forum, *Measurement of National-Level Logistics Costs and Performance,* Discussion Paper 2012.04, Figure 12, p. 46, www.internationaltransportforum.org/jtrc/DiscussionPapers/DP201204.pdf (1.75 MB); and Logistics Management, *23rd Annual State of Logistics Report,* p. 28, www.logisticsmgmt.com/images/site/LM1207_CovStateofLogistics_Rail.pdf (958 KB).

[59] Those test results also apply to commodity demand elasticities, which only enter the model multiplied by transport cost shares, and vice versa.

[60] The adjustments are as follows: In all short-haul markets, and in markets where all freight is carried by a single mode, all mode elasticities were reduced by 75 percent to prevent the model from predicting unlikely mode shifts. For the several long-haul routes identified by the logistic regression, elasticities were reduced by 20 percent.

Table 7.
Sensitivity Analyses

Policy Effect:	AEC Tax (Avg Result)	Likely Range†	Estimated Effect of AEC Tax in 2007					
			Test 1	Test 2	Test 3	Test 4	Test 5	Test 6
			Double RR Acc Risk	No Dray or Lift Costs	Alter-nate Elast's	Trim High Elast's	Trk Rates ×0.95	Trk Rates ×1.05
Avg Pct Diff. (Truck Tax vs External Cost)	17.0	4.1 — 28.2	16.9	16.2	16.2	16.3	16.5	16.5
Avg Pct Diff. (RR Tax vs External Cost)	15.9	3.4 — 27.2	15.1	14.9	16.3	15.1	15.3	16.1
Change, external costs (%)	-3.3	(-3.0) — (-3.5)	-2.0	-3.7	-2.7	-2.3	-3.6	-3.0
Fuel savings (%)	2.9	2.6 — 3.2	2.0	3.3	2.5	2.1	3.2	2.6
Tax revenue (billions of 2014 $)	68	68 — 69	73	68	69	69	68	69
Shift, ton-miles: truck to RR (%)	3.6	3.4 — 3.8	2.1	4.1	2.9	2.2	4.1	3.2
Market Contraction, total tons shipped (%)	-0.8	(-0.8) — (-0.8)	-0.8	-1.0	-0.8	-0.8	-0.8	-0.7
Reduction, truck trips (millions)	-3.2	(-3.1) — (-3.3)	-2.5	-4.7	-3.0	-2.5	-3.4	-3.0
Increase, rail-car trips (millions)	0.8	0.8 — 0.8	0.5	1.1	0.5	0.4	0.9	0.7
% Reduction, truck trips (truckload)	-1.2	(-1.1) — (-1.2)	-0.9	-1.9	-1.0	-0.9	-1.2	-1.1
% Increase, railcar trips (carload)	8.4	8.0 — 8.8	5.4	11.3	5.4	4.7	9.2	7.6
% Reduction, truck trips (bulk)	-1.7	(-1.7) — (-1.7)	-1.6	-1.7	-3.0	-1.7	-1.7	-1.6
% Change, railcar trips (bulk)	-0.1	(-0.0) — (-0.1)	-0.3	0.0	3.5	-0.1	0.0	-0.1
% Reduction, truck trips (intermodal)	-1.8	(-1.8) — (-1.9)	-1.2	-2.6	-1.0	-1.1	-2.0	-1.7
% Increase, railcar trips (intermodal)	11.3	10.6 — 11.9	6.2	14.8	4.3	5.1	12.6	10.1
% Reduction, truck trips (auto transport)	-1.7	(-1.6) — (-1.8)	-1.6	-1.7	-4.1	-1.7	-1.8	-1.6
% Increase, railcar trips (auto transport)	3.6	3.2 — 4.1	3.1	3.6	16.3	3.7	3.9	3.5

Note: †= In 1,000 iterations of the simulation model, two-thirds of the model's predictions lay within this range. [On March 31, 2015, CBO corrected several values in this column.]

Appendix:
Data and Parameter Values

The most important elements of the freight policy simulation model are the data on overland freight shipments in the United States, estimates of external costs and freight shipping rates, and demand responses to changes in price. External costs are discussed in the body of this paper. The other three elements are examined here, followed by other parameters of the model.

Freight Shipments

The freight data used in the analysis come from an extensive database of domestic freight movements called the Freight Analysis Framework (FAF), developed by the Federal Highway Administration (FHWA). Based primarily on the Commodity Flow Survey of 2007 (conducted as part of the Census Bureau's five-year Economic Census), FAF reports estimated one-year total freight flows within the United States, by origin, destination, commodity, and mode of transport.[61] The data set comprises nearly 76,000 observations, gathered from 48 states (Alaska and Hawaii are excluded) plus the District of Columbia and for 39 types of commodities. It includes domestic freight as well as the domestic transport of imported freight and of exports in transit to their exit port. The 2007 data were the most recent available at the time the analysis in this paper was completed—the results of the 2012 Commodity Flow Survey were published in December 2014. One advantage of the 2007 data is that they are not affected by the recession of 2008–2009 or the gradual economic recovery that followed.

The analysis assembles all of the FAF data pertaining to freight movements by truck, rail, and "multiple modes"—primarily, but not exclusively, intermodal freight that travels by truck and rail.[62] The analysis excludes FAF data on waterway, pipeline, and air freight. The FAF rail data do not include freight carried by small railroads terminating fewer than 4,500 carloads per year (less than 1 percent of total rail freight). FAF also does not include truck freight—primarily local deliveries—that does not travel over the National Highway System of Interstate, U.S., and state highways. Finally, the data do not include certain

---

[61] Freight Analysis Framework, www.ops.fhwa.dot.gov/freight/freight_analysis/faf/. The Commodity Flow Survey underlying the FAF data includes more than 100,000 sampled establishments, each of which reports on every shipment of freight it makes during four 1-week periods over the course of the sample year. See www.rita.dot.gov/bts/help_with_data/commodity_flow_survey.html.

[62] In the Commodity Flow Survey, intermodal freight is coded as having been shipped by "multiple modes and mail," rather than specifically by truck, rail, barge, or air. According to FAF, "[the term] 'intermodal' typically refers to containerized cargo that moves between ship and surface modes or between truck and rail, [although] repeated efforts to identify containerized cargo in the Commodity Flow Survey have proved unsuccessful." Because intermodal freight is a substantial line of business for the rail industry, the analysis classifies all such freight as having been shipped by rail and then drayed by truck to its final destination (over distances of up to several hundred miles). In the analysis, "multiple modes" usually refers to truck and rail, with most of the shipping by rail. That definition somewhat overstates rail market shares because some multimode shipments travel mostly by barge (and very little, in ton-mile terms, by air—around 0.06 percent in FAF). Also according to FAF, "The 'mail' component of 'multiple modes and mail' recognizes that shippers who use parcel delivery services typically do not know what modes were involved after the shipment was picked up." See Federal Highway Administration, *Freight Analysis Framework 3 User Guide* (June 2012), p. 6, www.ops.fhwa.dot.gov/freight/freight_analysis/faf/faf3/userguide/faf3_guide.pdf (1.9 MB).

types of domestic, trucked freight (for example agricultural, logging, construction, and retail shipping), although FAF adjusts for those omissions.[63]

FAF provides three measures of freight transport: tons, ton-miles, and cargo value. Because the external costs of freight transport arise from hauling freight over distances, ton-miles is the relevant measure for the analysis. Trucks produce the majority of the ton-miles in intermodal transport (modular shipping containers), carload/truckload transport (big-rig tractor trailers and rail boxcars), and automobile transport, although rail produces more ton-miles in some city-pair markets. Rail produces more ton-miles of bulk freight, a category that includes cereal grains, coal, minerals, and metallic ores. (See Table A-1 for aggregate totals.)[64]

Trucks (49.6 percent) and rail (42.9 percent) account for more than 92 percent of the ton-miles in the FAF data. The omitted modes of waterway, pipeline, and air freight, as well as "other," account for 5.5 percent, 0.1 percent, 0.1 percent, and 1.9 percent of the ton-miles, respectively. Waterway freight is largely barge conveyance of bulk agricultural grains, petroleum products, and rock and mineral commodities along inland and intracoastal waterways. (Barges actually account for an estimated 14 percent of intercity freight ton-miles in the United States, according to the Department of Transportation. If so, as much as a fifth of the ton-miles that this analysis counts as rail transport may have involved both barge and rail.)[65] Pipeline freight is primarily oil and petroleum products. Air freight has high value-to-weight ratios but is comparatively unimportant in ton-mile terms.

Among individual states, California and Texas, the two most populous states, rank second and third, respectively, in ton-miles of freight originated and first and second in tons and total value of freight. California is the locus of the nation's largest port complex (the Ports of Los Angeles and Long Beach), and Texas originates large amounts of chemicals and plastics. (See Table A-2 for the top 10 states by ton-miles originated.) Wyoming ranks first in ton-miles and seventh in tons—largely because of coal shipments from the Powder River Basin—but 48th in cargo value. In untabulated sensitivity testing, excluding Wyoming from the analysis (because very little coal would shift from rail to truck) left the results essentially unchanged.

Although trucks carry substantial amounts of freight on long-haul routes, their market shares are greatest on short-haul routes of 500 miles or less, which they can cover in a single day. (See Table A-3 for truck and rail market shares by length of haul and type of service. In that table, truck shares can be calculated as 100 minus rail share.) Rail usually provides slower service in short-haul markets because it can take a day or more to organize and assemble a train out of individual railcars headed for the same location. (Some short-haul routes, such as the 170-mile Seattle–Portland corridor, are well-served by regional freight rail.) However, trucks' time advantage begins to dissipate on longer routes because of truckers' work-hour limitations. On longer routes, rail can have a substantial advantage in labor costs per ton-mile: A freight train hauling 150 intermodal containers can be operated by two people with no overnight stops. To haul the same amount of freight by truck, without overnight stops, would require 300 drivers.

---

[63] Oak Ridge National Laboratory, *The Freight Analysis Framework, Version 3: Overview of the FAF3 National Freight Flow Tables* (October 28, 2010), pp. 13–24, http://faf.ornl.gov/fafweb/Documentation.aspx.

[64] Assignment of commodities to service types is based on Table A.3, "FAF Commodity Assignment to Rail Service Type," in American Association of Railroads, *National Rail Freight Infrastructure Capacity and Investment Study* (report prepared by Cambridge Systematics, September 2007), www.camsys.com/pubs/AAR_Nat_%20Rail_Cap_Study.pdf (5.25 MB).

[65] That is, 8 percentage points—the approximate difference between 14 percent and 5.5 percent—out of rail's 42.8 percent market share. See www.marad.dot.gov/documents/water_works_REV.pdf (6.9 MB)

Table A-1.
Freight Transport, by Service Type and Transport Mode, 2007
(Billions of ton-miles)

Service Type	Transport Mode			Service Type Total	Fraction of Grand Total
	Truck	Rail	Other		
Carload/Truckload	1,192	543	102	1,837	41%
Market Share	65%	30%	6%		
Bulk	508	1,176	205	1,889	43%
Market Share	27%	62%	11%		
Intermodal	438	142	19	599	14%
Market Share	73%	24%	3%		
Auto Transport	60	36	6	102	2%
Market Share	59%	35%	6%		
Total	**2,198**	**1,897**	**332**	**4,427**	

Note: Leading types of freight by service type: carload/truckload (base-metal articles, base metals, nonmetallic mineral products, other foodstuffs, basic chemicals); bulk (coal, nonmetallic minerals, metallic ores, animal feed, cereal grains); intermodal (machinery, textiles/leather, plastics/rubber, furniture, electronics).

Table A-2.
Total Overland Truck and Rail Freight, by State of Origin, 2007

Origin	N*	Ton-Miles (Billions)	RR Share (%)	Tons (Millions)	Value (Billions of 2007 dollars)	Ton-Mile Rank
Wyoming	1,526	548	98	512	19	1
California	1,738	328	25	1,114	1,763	2
Texas	1,745	292	35	1,089	1,164	3
Illinois	1,737	200	49	726	718	4
Minnesota	1,716	151	63	389	260	5
Florida	1,645	130	28	705	599	6
Kentucky	1,585	117	67	378	233	7
Pennsylvania	1,677	116	25	557	545	8
Ohio	1,658	114	31	544	590	9
New York	1,720	106	22	471	771	10

Note: N* = Number of observations. Each pertains to one type of commodity and one origin-destination state pair— for instance, total ton-miles of coal shipped from Wyoming to Georgia would constitute one observation.

Table A-3.
Rail Market Shares, by Length of Haul, 2007

Type of Service	Length of Haul*	N	Billions of Ton-Miles†	Average Rail Share (%)
Carload/Truckload	Short	6,630	726	12
	Long	27,187	1,010	45
Bulk	Short	2,354	619	32
	Long	6,491	1,065	92
Intermodal	Short	5,544	146	8
	Long	25,399	435	30
Auto Transport	Short	398	19	10
	Long	1,917	78	44

Notes: * = Short is less than 500 miles; long is 500 miles or more.

Average lengths of short- and long-haul routes are around 270 miles and 1,425 miles, respectively.

† = Total long-haul ton-miles are only two to four times greater than short-haul ton-miles despite much longer routes (five or six times longer) and many more markets (the number N of commodity/state-pair markets is three to five times greater for long haul). That is because short-haul activity only occurs within a state and with its nearest neighbors (fewer possible markets) and because the number of short-haul trips (not shown in the table) is greater.

Evidence for rail's comparative advantages on long-haul routes is evident in its average market shares, which are three to four times greater than they are on short-haul routes. Rail's ton-mile share of bulk freight is more than 90 percent on long hauls. For especially long routes of more than 1,500 miles, rail market shares are higher than those in Table A-3: For bulk and carload service, rail shares are only a little higher, but for intermodal and auto-transport service, rail shares on routes of more than 1,500 miles are 35 percent and 52 percent, respectively, versus 30 percent and 44 percent in Table A-3.

Most types of freight are carried almost exclusively by truck or rail. (See Figure A-1 for the total ton-miles for each of the 39 types of freight in the FAF data and the share of those ton-miles hauled by rail, truck, or other modes.) For the most prominent exceptions—cereal grains, gravel, basic chemicals, and "other agricultural products"—river barges traveling along the Mississippi River system are responsible for most of the remaining ton-miles. But even for those commodities, truck and rail are responsible for a large majority of the ton-miles. (The analysis excludes those freight types—crude petroleum, gasoline, and fuel oils—that travel primarily by pipeline.) Thus, restricting the analysis to truck and rail transport does not significantly limit the applicability of the results except in regional markets with substantial barge service.

The commodities for which rail's market shares are lowest tend to have relatively few total ton-miles. That is, for commodities for which truck ton-miles are particularly high, rail appears to be a viable alternative (although individual markets vary in how well-served they are by rail).

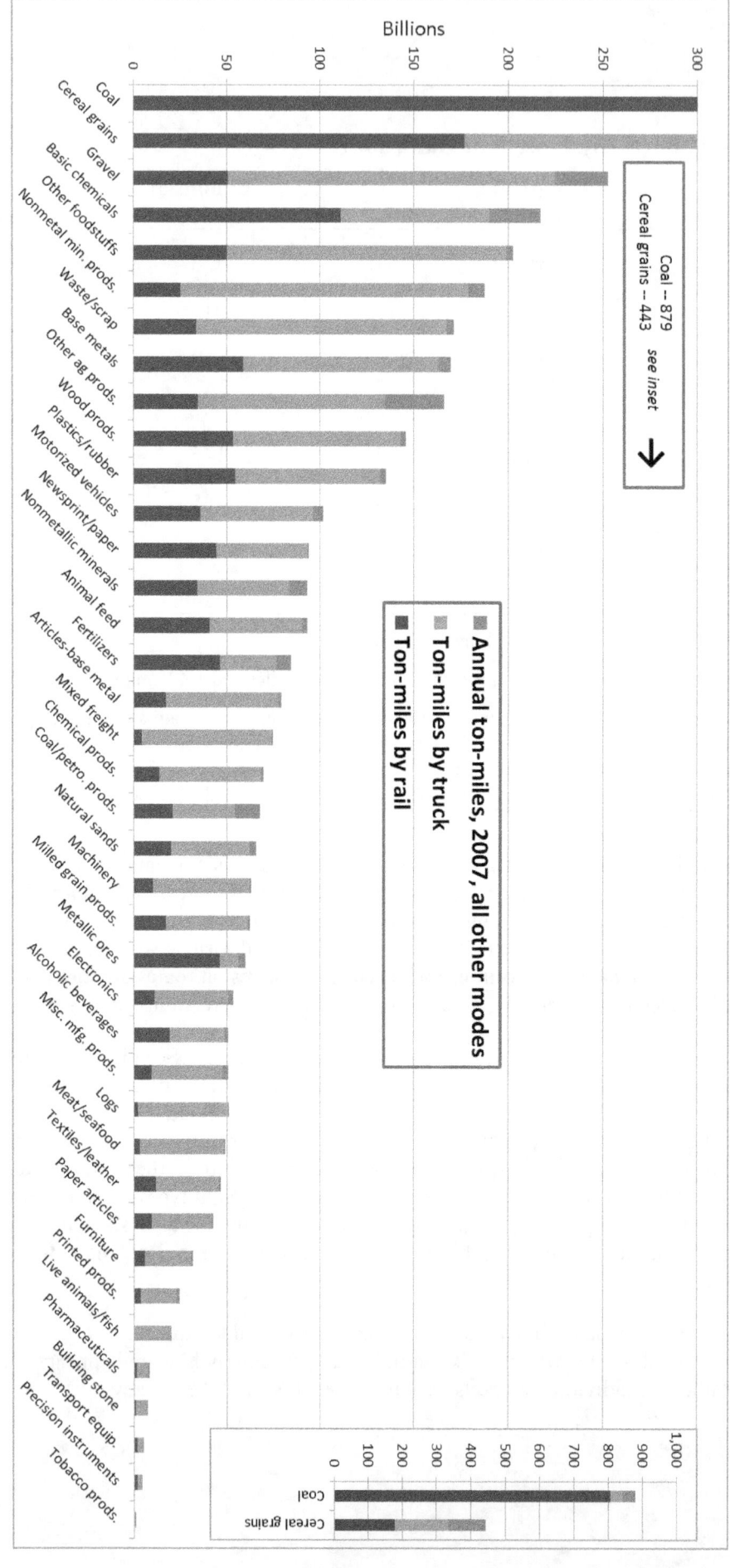

Figure A-1.
Annual Freight Transport, by Type and Mode, 2007
(Billions of ton-miles)

34

Table A-4.
Average Shipping Rates
(Cents per ton-mile)

Service Type	Truck	Rail
Carload/Truckload	14.6 (3.4)	4.7 (2.3)
Bulk	13.6 (1.4)	3.5 (1.2)
Intermodal	17.4 (4.2)	5.6 (2.2)
Auto Transport	13.8 (2.4)	9.6 (4.3)
Total	**15.6** **(3.9)**	**5.1** **(2.5)**

Notes: Averages are not weighted by miles or by ton-miles.

The "Total" category reports averages over individual observations, not over the service-type averages.

Values in parentheses are standard deviations.

Shipping Rates

Shipping rates (or prices) play a crucial role in this analysis. Whatever a mode's external costs, adding those costs to its rates will have less of an impact on shippers' mode choices the higher those rates are to begin with. Mathematically, higher shipping rates imply lower percentage increases: A high tax on high-cost shipping could therefore mean a smaller percentage increase than a lower tax on lower-cost shipping. Higher shipping rates also mean shippers value the service more. Shipping rates for trucked freight are higher, on average, than rail rates. (See Table A-4.) Thus, although average external costs per ton-mile are greater for trucking than for rail—more than six times higher, on net, according to the values in Table 1—an external-cost tax on freight shipments would not affect trucking six times more than rail.

The rail rates in the analysis come from public data provided by the Surface Transportation Board (STB), a federal agency charged by the Congress with auditing Class I railroads.[66] The STB publishes representative rail shipping rates for different classes of service. This analysis uses the average rates for 2007 from the STB's *Study of Railroad Rates: 1985–2007.*[67] The source for the truck rates used in the simulations, FHWA's Intermodal Transportation and Inventory Costing model, is described in the sensitivity analysis.

---

[66] Seven Class I freight railroads operate in the United States: BNSF, CSX, Grand Trunk (owned by Canadian National), and Kansas City Southern, Norfolk Southern, Soo Line (owned by Canadian Pacific), and Union Pacific. In 2011, those railroads accounted for about 69 percent of industry freight rail mileage and 94 percent of total rail freight revenue. See Association of American Railroads, *An Overview of America's Freight Railroads* (July 2012), www.aar.org.

[67] Surface Transportation Board, Office of Economics, Environmental Analysis & Administration, Section of Economics (January 16, 2009), www.stb.dot.gov/stb/docs/Rate%20Studies/Post%20Rate%20Study.xlsx

Lacking data on actual payloads, this analysis uses an average payload factor of 53 percent so that the resulting shipping rates equal, on average, the 2007 average truckload-sector shipping rate in the *National Transportation Statistics*.[68] The effect of using different truck rates is examined in the sensitivity analysis.

The shipping rates reported in Table A-4 are averages over a range that varies by route distance. Freight haulers can charge lower rates on longer routes because the fixed costs of loading and unloading can be spread over more revenue-miles. As with other parameters in the simulation model, actual shipping rates for each simulation are drawn from probability distributions that reflect uncertainty and variation in the source data.

Demand Responses

The model performs multiple iterations for each policy simulation. In each iteration, after the model has selected new values for prices and external costs from their respective probability ranges and has applied the simulated policy by calculating new prices, the next step is to predict how customers will respond to the price changes. Customers will ship slightly less freight and will shift some of their business, where feasible, to the mode whose prices have gone up less. That mode is usually rail.

The parameters that capture those responses are own-price elasticities of demand for the commodities being shipped and cross-price elasticities of mode choice. The own-price elasticities determine effects on total shipping: When transport prices change (as a result of a new policy, for instance), the simulation model calculates the change in demand for a commodity as $(\eta \times C \times T)$, where η is the own-price elasticity of demand for the commodity; C is the percentage change in its shipping cost (from the change in transport prices) in a particular market, including any changes to drayage (truck delivery) costs if shipping by rail; and T is the transport cost share of that commodity's total production and distribution costs. C is a calculated value; T and η are model parameters. For most commodities, $(T \times C \times \eta)$ implies a decrease of less than 1 percent in total ton-miles.

The more substantial policy effect is on shippers' mode choices, which depend on the cross-price elasticities. When transport prices change, the price for one mode relative to the other also changes. The percentage of ton-miles that switches modes in response is calculated (for each combination of origin, destination, and commodity) as

$$\exp(\varepsilon_{r,d} \times \ln[(1+C_d)/(1+C_r)]) \approx R_c \times \varepsilon_{r,d},$$

where R_c is the relative change in total shipping costs for one mode versus the other, and $\varepsilon_{r,d}$ is the cross-price elasticity of the "receiving" mode (usually rail) with respect to the "donating" mode (usually truck). The expression inside $\ln[\bullet]$ is the percentage increase in the total cost to ship (a commodity on a route) by the donating mode relative to the receiving mode, based on their respective absolute percentage increases C_d and C_r. The "exp" and "ln" refer to the exponential and logarithmic functions e^x and $\log_e(x)$, respectively, where e is the mathematical constant approximately equal to 2.72. So, if truck shipping costs increased by 10 percent relative to rail for a particular commodity on a particular route, and if the cross-

---

[68] Department of Transportation, Bureau of Transportation Statistics, Table 4-21, "Average Freight Revenue per Ton-Mile" (entry for 2007), www.rita.dot.gov/bts/sites/rita.dot.gov.bts/files/publications/national_transportation_statistics/index.html. The value in Table 4-21 is an average rate for both the "truckload" and the higher cost "less-than-truckload" segments of the trucking industry. (It is the truckload segment that competes with rail.) If the truck rates used in the simulation model had been lower, the policy effects it estimated would have been slightly greater.

price elasticity was 0.5, rail ton-miles for that commodity on that route would increase by exp(0.5 × ln[1.1]) = 1.049, or 4.9 percent.[69]

The truck/rail mode-choice elasticities in the simulation model come from the research literature.[70] They indicate that the demand for transport of bulk commodities and raw materials is inelastic and that the transport demand for finished goods can be very elastic. (See Table A-5.) For example, for "bulk farm products," a 10 percent relative increase in truck shipping costs would increase rail shipping of those commodities by 0.2 percent to 0.3 percent. For coal, the shift would be 1.4 percent to 1.9 percent, based on "bulk, all else." For furniture, by contrast, if the cost to ship by truck rose by 10 percent relative to rail, rail's ton-miles of furniture shipping would increase by 40 percent to 47 percent. The elasticities for finished goods are all much greater than one, indicating that truck and rail compete intensely for finished-goods business.

Other Parameters

The freight ton-miles, shipping rates, and mode-choice elasticities described above are central to the calculation of policy effects. The parameters and data elements described below, although an important determinant of total shipping costs, either play only a secondary role in the policy-effect calculations or would not be directly altered by a change in freight policy.

Drayage and Lift Costs. For many rail freight deliveries, drayage is necessary to carry a shipment of cargo from the transfer station or railhead (where the rail car is unloaded) to the final destination (where the consignee awaits the shipment). Drayage costs can constitute a significant fraction of the total cost of shipping by rail.[71] In a 2007 study published by the Transportation Research Board, drayage costs were said to vary between $50 and $500 per trip, depending on the length of the dray.[72] That study characterized $150 as a "typical" cost per container or trailer.

This analysis adopts those values, drawing drayage costs from a triangular distribution with minimum, modal, and maximum values of $50, $150, and $500. Costs are drawn independently for each shipment of intermodal or carload freight. In the simulations, trains deliver all bulk freight and motor vehicles directly to the final destination; no drayage is necessary in those cases.[73]

For the drayage segments of any rail freight delivery, the simulation model charges the external costs associated with trucking to the overall rail external costs for that trip. That is, external-cost pricing will

---

[69] The model does not allow any change in total ton-miles as a result of mode switching: For each market, the model calculates the number of ton-miles gained by the receiving mode and then subtracts that number from the donating mode. Where the receiving mode has a large market share, its percentage gain can translate into more ton-miles than the donating mode has to give. In such cases, the model limits gains to the donating mode's total ton-miles.

[70] Transportation Research Board, National Cooperative Highway Research Program, *A Guidebook for Forecasting Freight Transportation Demand,* NCHRP Report 388, National Academy Press (1997), Appendix G: "Rail/Truck Modal Diversion," pp. 130–135. Those estimated mode-choice elasticities were estimated for Canadian railways operating in the United States and Canada.

[71] Nam Seok Kim and Bert Van Wee, "The Relative Importance of Factors That Influence the Break-Even Distance of Intermodal Freight Transport Systems," *Journal of Transport Geography,* vol.19 (2011), pp. 859–875.

[72] Joseph Bryan and others, *Rail Freight Solutions to Roadway Congestion—Final Report and Guidebook,* National Cooperative Highway Research Program Report 586 (Transportation Research Board, National Academies of Science, 2007), p. G-81.

[73] In one variant of the simulations, a short portside dray was also included, to convey imported goods from dock to initial railhead. Because the portside drays are relatively short in those simulations, the conclusions were not affected. Those results are not presented here.

Table A-5.
Mode-Choice Elasticities

Table Removed Due to Copyright Restrictions

Source: J. Jones, F. Nix, and C. Schwier, *The Impact of Changes in Road User Charges on Canadian Railways,* (report prepared for Transport Canada by the Canadian Institute of Guided Ground Transport, Kingston, Ontario, September 1990), Table 5.2, as cited in National Cooperative Highway Research Program, Report 388: *A Guidebook for Forecasting Freight Transportation Demand* (Transportation Research Board, National Academy Press, Washington, DC, 1997), p. 131.

make each drayage more costly, according to the external costs of trucking. But those costs are paid by rail customers.

The simulation model also adds costs associated with lifting a shipping container onto a railcar or truck trailer. The costs are the same for either mode, varying between $50 and $150 per lift. For intermodal and carload/truckload freight, the model randomly draws lift costs from a uniform distribution over that range, at both the beginning and the end of the journey, and adds it to the total cost of the trip.[74]

---

[74] Only some types of carload or truckload freight require a lift. In cases in which no lift is required, the "lift" cost can be interpreted as an unloading cost. Adding that cost to carload/truckload freight is equivalent to using higher unloading costs than for bulk freight or motor-vehicle deliveries, because the simulation model does not add lift costs for that type of freight. For terminal (lift) costs, see National Cooperative Highway Research Program Report 586. Other studies have estimated lift costs of $140 (see J.E. Barton and others, "Developing a Proposal for a Multi-user Intermodal Freight Terminal as a Public-Private Partnership: Lessons Learned About Public and Private Perspectives, Timing, and Roles," *Transportation Research Record 1659* (1999), pp. 145–151), and of $30 (see

Transport Share of Production and Distribution Costs. The transport cost share data in the simulation model come from the Transportation Satellite Accounts (TSA) developed jointly by the Bureau of Transportation Statistics and the Bureau of Economic Analysis.[75] The most recent version, published in

2011, contains data for 1997. The transport cost shares in the simulation model exclude costs relating to transport by air or by pipeline and include expenditures for in-house transportation.[76] (See Table A-6.)

Elasticities of Commodity Demand. When transport costs increase, the effect on freight-transport demand depends on how much the increases raise commodity prices and how much those higher prices, in turn, reduce total commodity sales. To estimate the market contractions that would result from the analyzed external-cost policies, the simulation model uses estimated price elasticities of demand for each commodity. There are few comprehensive, internally consistent sources for such estimates. The values in the simulation model come, primarily, from a recent study on the impacts that carbon dioxide prices might have on U.S. industrial output.[77] For several commodities in this analysis that were not included in that study, the model uses estimates from other recent, industry-specific research, including the Congressional Budget Office's research. (See Table A-6.) In general, freight types with higher transportation cost shares have smaller elasticities.

Route Distance. Freight shipments in the FAF data are measured in annual total ton-miles from the state of origin to the state of destination, including intrastate totals. For route distance, which the simulation model uses to estimate trip costs and the total annual number of shipments for each mode and each state pair, the model takes the average shipping distances estimated in the Commodity Flow Survey over the routes connecting each state pair.[78] Route distance is an estimate of the average distance traveled on the actual routes (highways and railways) that exist between each pair of states. For a few state pairs, the number of shipments in 2007 was sufficiently low that FAF could not report average shipping distances without violating shippers' confidentiality, so no distance estimate was prepared. For those pairs, the arc distances (straight-line distances, accounting for the earth's curvature) between large metropolitan areas in each of those states are used, expanded by 15 percent to reflect the average relationship between arc distance and estimated route distance in the other state pairs.

Circuity and Empty Return Rates. Circuity is the extent to which rail routes tend to be longer than truck routes between the same city pairs. In the simulations, rail routes are up to 10 percent more circuitous than truck routes, via a circuity parameter whose value is drawn at random (with equal

---

Randolph Resor and James Blaze, "Short-Haul Rail Intermodal: Can It Compete With Trucks?" *Transportation Research Record 1873* (2004), pp. 45–52.)

[75] Department of Transportation, Bureau of Transportation Statistics, *Transportation Satellite Accounts: A Look at Transportation's Role in the Economy, 2011*, Appendix Table 4, "TSA Detailed Commodity-by-Industry Direct Requirements: 1997," www.rita.dot.gov/bts/sites/rita.dot.gov.bts/files/publications/transportation_satellite_accounts/2011/index.html.

[76] The commodities in the TSA are classified according to the North American Industrial Classification System, which only approximately corresponds to the freight classifications in the FAF shipping data. The author matched the TSA estimates to the FAF data using a correspondence provided with the FAF data, available at ops.fhwa.dot.gov/freight/freight_analysis/faf/faf2_reports/reports8/s5_naics.htm.

[77] Except where noted in Table A-6, elasticity estimates come from Mun S. Ho, Richard Morgenstern, and Jhih-Shyang Shih, *Impact of Carbon Price Policies on U.S. Industry*, RFF Discussion Paper 08-37 (Resources for the Future, 2008), Table B6, "Demand Elasticity for Output," pp. 86–87.

[78] Department of Transportation, Bureau of Transportation Statistics, *How Freight Moves: Estimating Mileage and Routes Using an Innovative GIS Tool*, www.rita.dot.gov/bts/sites/rita.dot.gov.bts/files/publications/bts_technical_report/june_2007/html/entire.html.

Table A-6.
Transport Cost Shares and Demand Elasticities

Freight Type	Transport Share	Elasticity	Freight Type	Transport Share	Elasticity
Live animals and fish	0.08	-0.81	Plastics and rubber	0.04	-0.99
Cereal grains (Including seed)	0.10	-0.81	Logs and other wood in the rough	0.11	-0.70
Other agricultural products	0.10	-0.81	Wood products	0.05	-0.70
Animal feed, products of animal origin n.e.c.*	0.04	-0.64	Pulp, newsprint, paper, and paperboard	0.04	-0.70
Meat/fish/seafood and their preparations	0.04	-0.64	Paper or paperboard articles	0.04	-1.66
Milled grain prods and preps, bakery products	0.04	-0.64	Printed products	0.03	-1.66
Other prepared foodstuffs, fats/ oils	0.04	-0.64	Textiles/leather and articles thereof	0.03	-1.14
Alcoholic beverages	0.04	-0.64	Nonmetallic mineral products	0.08	-0.83
Tobacco products	0.02	-0.42†	Base metal in primary/semifinished forms, and in finished basic shapes	0.03	-0.95
Monumental or building stone	0.11	-0.83	Articles of base metal	0.03	-0.50
Natural sands	0.11	-0.83	Machinery	0.02	-1.66
Gravel and crushed stone	0.11	-0.83	Electronic and other electrical eqpt/components, office eqpt	0.01	-2.60
Non-metallic minerals, n.e.c.	0.11	-0.83	Motorized and other vehicles, including parts	0.02	-2.48
Metallic ores and concentrates	0.09	-0.63	Transportation equipment n.e.c.	0.02	-2.48
Coal	0.22	-0.11	Precision instruments and apparatus	0.02	-1.66
Other coal and petroleum products n.e.c.	0.02	-0.11	Furniture, mattresses/supports, lamps and lighting fittings,illuminated signs	0.04	-0.70
Basic chemicals	0.03	-0.99	Misc. manufacturing products **	0.03	-1.66
Pharmaceutical products	0.01	-0.30‡	Waste/scrap	0.01	-0.74
Fertilizers	0.06	-0.99	Mixed freight: grocery, conv. store, restaurant foods/supplies; hardware/plumbing/office supplies	0.03	-1.66
Chemical products and preparations n.e.c.	0.03	-0.99			

Notes: Data sources given in the text. Where commodity types in FAF did not match those in the table, the author assigned elasticities and travel cost shares from similar categories.

* = n.e.c. = not elsewhere classified.

** = Author applied the elasticity estimate for "misc. manufacturing products" to the following categories lacking an estimate in Ho and others: "paper or paperboard articles," "printed products," "precision instruments," and "mixed freight."

† = From Department of Health and Human Services, Centers for Disease Control and Prevention, *Reducing Tobacco Use: A Report of the Surgeon General* (2000), p. 329. CBO cited a range from -0.3 to -0.7 in Congressional Budget Office, *Raising the Excise Tax on Cigarettes: Effects on Health and the Federal Budget* (June 2012), p. 8, www.cbo.gov/publication/43319.

‡ = Congressional Budget Office, *Issues in Designing a Prescription Drug Benefit for Medicare* (October 2002), p. 36, www.cbo.gov/publication/14182.

Table A-7.
Empty Miles as a Percentage of Total Miles, by Mode and Type of Equipment

Table Removed Due to Copyright Restrictions

likelihood for any value from 10 percent to 20 percent) before each iteration of the model. That variation in circuity contributes to uncertainty in model outputs as expressed in the likely range in Table 7. For that reason, the circuity parameter is not subjected to sensitivity testing. In addition, in a 2011 study, the Government Accountability Office concluded that it "could not find evidence to suggest that [differences in rail route circuity] are large enough to change the direction or the order of magnitude of our findings" regarding rail's external costs.[79]

Although the analysis is conducted in terms of ton-miles of freight, it implicitly accounts for empty return miles as well. To maximize profits, trucking and railroad companies would seek to minimize empty repositioning miles. In any case, they set their rates to recover, on average, their costs for any such travel. Likewise, the external-cost parameters in the simulation model, although expressed in costs per ton-mile, reflect estimates of total costs, including costs associated with empty return miles. Thus, although the simulated policies only assess laden (freight-transport) miles, the policies fully internalize the costs of empty returns as well. That is particularly true of policies that, in actual application, would apply to both laden and empty miles: taxes on fuel, truck tires, and vehicle miles traveled.[80] Available data suggest that both modes engage in roughly similar amounts of such travel. (See Table A-7.)

Tax Pass-Through Rate. Because railroad companies have high fixed costs to build a network of tracks, their potential to enter a market is limited. In the simulation model, the railroad industry (in contrast to the trucking industry) is not perfectly competitive. As a result, increasing the supply of rail transport services beyond a certain point is likely to involve rising marginal costs. If current rail industry supply is near that

---

[79] Government Accountability Office, *Surface Freight Transportation: A Comparison of the Costs of Road, Rail, and Waterways Freight Shipments That Are Not Passed on to Consumers,* GAO-11-134 (January 26, 2011), p. 21, www.gao.gov/products/GAO-11-134

[80] In translating the tire tax—the sole policy in the analysis that is not based on estimated external costs—into per-ton-mile terms, an empty-return rate of 30 percent is used, meaning that 3 of every 10 truck miles is driven without any payload.

point, the aggregate rail supply curve could be upward-sloping (as rising marginal costs increase the slope of the supply curve). In that case, if policymakers adopted a tax on freight transport, railroad companies would find it profitable to pay a portion of the tax themselves rather than passing the entire tax along to their shippers. (Figure 1 showed that firms in competitive industries like trucking will pass the full tax along to their customers.) The tax pass-through rate is the portion of the tax that the shippers pay.

This analysis has no data on freight-haulers' actual pass-through rates. For trucking companies, the simulation model uses a pass-through rate of 1.0 (truck shippers pay the full tax). For rail, the model uses a pass-through rate of between 0.9 and 1.0, with an average value of 0.95—meaning that rail shippers pay, on average, 95 percent of any tax. Values farther from 1.0 make rail more attractive to shippers than it otherwise would be when a tax is applied, because the lower pass-through rate reduces the shippers' share of the tax. For each iteration of the model, a value is drawn at random from that range. That uncertainty helps widen the model's prediction interval (or likely range); the pass-through rate is not subjected to sensitivity testing.

Payload Capacities. To estimate the number of railcar or truck trips per year—the latter is correlated with highway congestion and accidents—and the number of drayage and lift operations, which factor into total trip costs, the analysis draws on two sets of average-payload estimates. Average truck payloads come from the Federal Highway Administration and average rail payloads come from the Surface Transportation Board. Each source provides two estimates per commodity type. In simulating a policy, the model randomly selects one of the estimates. Through repetition, the simulations reflect the average truck and rail payload values reported below. (See Table A-8.)

Alternate Mode-Choice Elasticity Estimates. This analysis considers two sets of detailed, carefully estimated mode-choice elasticities for truck versus rail. One set is used for the primary analysis; the effect of that choice is tested by using the other set in a sensitivity analysis. The alternate set comes from an often-cited study on U.S. overland freight shipments. It includes both national and regional estimates, although for broader commodity categories than in the set used in the primary analysis.[81] (See Table A-9.) To make use of those estimates, this analysis assigns each of the 39 FAF commodities to one of the eight commodity groups in Table A-9, based on the descriptions in the first column.

The estimates in Table A-9 imply much more price sensitivity for bulk-commodity transport than do the estimates in Table A-5. For a commodity like coal, for example, it would be problematic if the price of rail transport increased by 10 percent and the mode-choice elasticity was 1.04 (as in Table A-9). Because rail's market share for coal transport is so great, the resulting 10 percent shift from rail to truck would overwhelm the available supply of trucks and drivers. No such price change occurs in the simulations— the rail price usually declines relative to the truck price—but that example shows that the alternate estimates do not allow for the captive shipping that exists in some markets. A virtue of the alternate estimates, however, is that none implies more than a 16 percent shift in response to a 10 percent change in one mode's price. By contrast, the largest elasticity in Table A-5 implies more than a 50 percent shift away from that mode (for transport of fabricated metals). As previously noted, in one sensitivity analysis the larger elasticities in Table A-5 are reduced so that they are more like those in Table A-9. Despite substantial differences in the two sets of elasticity estimates, the sensitivity analysis shows that they both support qualitatively similar conclusions.

---

[81] Walid M. Abdelwahab, "Elasticities of Mode Choice Probabilities and Market Elasticities of Demand: Evidence From a Simultaneous Mode Choice/Shipment-Size Freight Transport Model," *Transportation Research Part E: Logistics and Transportation Review*, vol. 34, no. 4 (1998), pp. 257–266.

Table A-8.
Average Payloads, by Mode and Commodity Type
(Tons)

Commodity Type	Truck Payload	Rail Payload
Service Category: Carload/Truckload		
Milled Grain Products	17.0	19.6
Other Food Products	17.9	70.7
Building Stone	16.1	24.3
Natural Sands, Clay, Concrete, Glass	14.4	95.0
Lumber or Wood Products	21.0	77.8
Pulp, Paper, Allied Products	18.6	53.8
Chemicals and Allied Products	16.9	87.0
Primary Metal Products	20.0	84.8
Fabricated Metal Products	14.3	15.2
Waste or Scrap Metals	16.0	66.4
Service Category: Bulk		
Agricultural Products	17.0	93.4
Coal	16.1	113.0
Metallic Ores	11.5	89.1
Gravel, Nonmetallic Minerals	16.1	99.1
Service Category: Intermodal		
Fresh Fish or Marine Products	12.6	29.2
Alcoholic Beverages	17.9	19.6
Tobacco Products	16.6	13.5
Textile Mill Products	16.3	13.0
Apparel or Related Products	12.4	12.9
Leather or Leather Products	11.2	13.6
Furniture or Fixtures	11.4	10.5
Printed Matter	13.8	17.5
Rubber or Miscellaneous Plastics	9.2	14.0
Machinery	10.8	28.3
Electrical Equipment	12.8	12.5
Other Transportation Equipment	11.3	21.2
Instruments, Photo & Optical Equipment	9.6	12.5
Mixed Freight, Misc. Manufactured Products	14.6	13.6
Service Category: Auto Transport		
Motorized Vehicles	11.3	21.2

Notes: Some of the 39 FAF commodity types are more narrowly defined than the 29 commodity types in this table; to address mismatches, the author assigned payload values for some commodity types from similar categories. Truck payloads are based on the average of "interstate" and "through-travel" truck load factors from Reebie and Associates. See Federal Highway Administration, *Quick Response Freight Manual II,* FHWA-HOP-08-010 (September 2007), Table 6-6, www.ops.fhwa.dot.gov/freight/publications/qrfm2/sect05.htm. Rail payloads are based on the average of (annual tonnage/annual rail carloads), 2008 and 2007, Carload Waybill Sample, *Reference Guide for the 2008 Surface Transportation Board Carload Waybill Sample,* Tables 1-7 and 1-9, pp. 11 and 13, www.stb.dot.gov/stb/docs/Waybill/2008%20STB%20Waybill%20Reference%20Guide_JN.pdf (1.1 MB).

www.ingramcontent.com/pod-product-compliance
Lightning Source LLC
Chambersburg PA
CBHW080619180526
45168CB00007B/2972